BOOM TOWN REFLECTIONS

VOLUME – 7

A DARK AND COLD PLACE

I0559315

By

Mark A. Gregg

An Imprint of Collins Publishing House

4900 California Ave, Bakersfield, CA 93309, USA

Collins's website address: www.collinspublishinghouse.com

First published in English by Collins Publishing House in 2024

1st Edition 2024

Mark A. Gregg © 2024

Mark A. Gregg asserts the moral right

to be identified as the author of this work.

A catalogue record for this book is available

from the Library of Congress United States.

LCCN: 2024924851

E Book ISBN: 978-1-966029-39-7

Paperback ISBN: 978-1-966029-40-3

Hardcover ISBN: 978-1-966029-41-0

Printed and bounded in United States of America.

All rights reserved. No part of this publication may be reproduced, distributed, or transmitted in any form or by any means, including photocopying, recording, or other electronic or mechanical methods, without the prior written permission of the publisher, except as permitted by U.S. copyright law.

For permission requests, contact
info@collinspublishinghouse.com

Table of Contents

CHAPTER 1

DESERET G & T

Our time in Columbia, Maryland was interesting and, for the most part, enjoyable. It was the miracle adoption of our son Joshua that will always overshadow any other event in Maryland. Now that our family was finally complete, we began longing for the west again. *Why?*

Wearing a suit and tie was not my calling. I didn't mind it all that much, but it certainly wasn't my first choice. While at Engineering Physics I dealt with a continuously perplexing conundrum; I was the happiest when I was working on a plant site but I was also the unhappiest because I had to be away from Vangie and the kids to do so. The answer was simple. I needed to find a way back into a power plant.

Don Pillar, a friend and former coworker at Bridger and Laramie River Station was now working as a Shift Supervisor at the Bonanza Plant in Vernal, Utah. I called, and we talked for a long time about the Bonanza facility. He filled me in on what was happening with the plant. He said the powerhouse was owned and operated by Deseret G&T (Generation and Transmission) and that they were headquartered in Salt Lake City. This plant was their first and only power plant. He had only worked there for a few months as he was hired right after they hired the current plant manager.

Don said that before he was hired, the plant had a rough start, and things were still "out of control." Deseret finally fired the original plant manager in an attempt to "correct the issues."

The Deseret upper management concluded they had a few too many former Utah Power and Light personnel who provided grossly myopic methods of running a power plant.

In their search for a new Plant Manager, they hired the current plant manager, a man named Bob Culligan. Don said he was a charming, witty, soft-spoken, bespectacled Tennessee boy in his mid to late 50s who had a long history of managing large and troublesome plants. I thanked Don for all his information and sent them a resume'.

Oddly, the Deseret personnel department contacted me *immediately* upon receiving my resume'. A gentleman named Rick Heller from Deseret's personnel department called, requesting me to come for an interview *as soon as possible*. I immediately acquiesced and took some vacation from EP.

I flew from BWI to Salt Lake City, where I rented a car and drove the scenic three-hour drive to Vernal. Vangie and I had been through Vernal many times when we lived in Rock Springs. Vernal was about 5,000 people and a ton of Mormon churches. However, the town itself was relatively clean for an eastern Utah town and seemed like a decent place to live. As far as I was concerned, it was much better than Delta, Utah.

I arrived in Vernal late on a Wednesday night and early Thursday morning, drove the sensory-numbing 38 miles into the geographical middle of *absolute nowhere* to get to the plant. The area where the plant sits is nothing but an extreme desert appearing to be void of any living thing as far as the eye can see.

I couldn't imagine why Deseret chose this area to build the plant. It was not even near the Green River, the only water source in the entire region. I found out later that the water to run the plant was piped in from a pump station on the Green River located over 20 miles away.

Bonanza Power Plant

Arriving at the plant excited me. Burns and McDonnell Engineering did the design, the construction management, and the commissioning. I felt they were one of the best in the business.

It appeared to be an extremely nice facility. It was a fully indoor unit, and the exterior was aesthetically pleasing. It was different shades of brown with floor-to-roof windows on each end of the large turbine deck. I immediately liked the look of the plant.

Unfortunately, my interview seemed brief and lacking substance. The receptionist led me into the large and opulent plant manager's office and introduced me to Bob Culligan, the plant manager. He had a thick head of wavy, graying hair with enough wrinkles to show wisdom but not enough to particularly look old. He seemed very intelligent and, unbeknownst to most people due to his charm, would eventually reveal a deeply sinister side. Stan Gorman, the Operations Superintendent, was also in attendance.

Bob did most of the talking. Though I was being interviewed for what was supposed to be a Shift Supervisor position, the entire interview concerned my views on training and training development.

Bob was deeply interested in what I was doing for Engineering Physics (EP). Based on the interview, I should have realized he had no interest in me as a shift supervisor.

At one point, he lowered his head and peered out of the top of his thick bifocals, pointedly saying, "Do you enjoy developing training material and technical writing?" Stan Gorman gave me the impression that he was puzzled by this line of questioning, but he seemed to play along. I was aware that they had two full-time trainers and technical writers on staff at the plant.

"Yes, I enjoy training development and technical writing a great deal," I answered confidently. What did he think I was going to say? That I hated it? Didn't he realize I was interviewing for a job that I wanted quite badly? I decided to reinforce my commitment to training and technical writing by adding, "The *ONLY* reason I want to leave Engineering Physics is because of the intense travel regimen. I really enjoy the job."

The interview was over in less than 30 minutes and certainly could have taken place over the phone. We shook hands, and I returned to Salt Lake City that afternoon.

I left there without a clue about whether they were interested in hiring me. Neither of them tipped their hats verbally or even with body language. The entire interview was odd and seemed to be a total waste of time.

I arrived home on Friday afternoon. I had the weekend off, so Vangie, the kids, and I enjoyed family time for a few days. Unfortunately, after my lackluster interview, I never expected a callback. However, Monday evening at about 6:00 pm, Rick Heller from Deseret's personnel department called.

Rick was a pleasant man and seemed gung-ho in fulfilling his duties to Deseret. He told me that Bob Culligan was quite impressed with my background and "my performance during the interview." *What??? My performance during the interview?* I was taken aback by the revelation that I apparently interviewed well. I thought it was a poor performance on *everyone's part*. Bob only asked a few pointed questions. Stan Gorman said very little and seemed perplexed. The entire process was over in less than a half hour.

Rick immediately offered me the position of dayshift shift supervisor at the Bonanza Power Plant. Hold on… Did he say *day shift, Shift Supervisor???* I was absolutely thrilled, but it didn't make sense. I was to be a dayshift-*only* Shift Supervisor.

I HATED shift work more than I could express without using a substantial string of vulgar metaphors. Being offered a technical, *DAY-SHIFT* position in a power plant was beyond my wildest dreams. The pay was substantially more than I was making at Engineering Physics, and the benefits were *even* better.

Rick finished the call by outlining the abundant benefits they offered. He explained that Deseret had an excellent moving package and would even buy our house if necessary. This, of course, was not necessary because we were still renting the same duplex we originally moved into after arriving in Columbia. However, they would also buy out the lease on the duplex if necessary.

If his job was to sell me on coming there, I took the bait… *Hook, line, and sinker!* It was a no-brainer to me. In a single, fifteen-minute phone call, I was propelled into the stratosphere of euphoria over being offered a *day-shift* position in a plant located out west that sounded like paradise power.

Unfortunately, Vangie was far less impressed about moving back to Utah. This didn't deter me in the least. I was offered a dayshift, technical-based power plant position in a plant out west near what we considered our home for more money and better benefits. This was truly the Holy Grail for me.

Instantly, I went into consummate sales mode with Vangie over this position. I had the energy and focus of a speeding freight train charging, out of control, down a mountain without brakes. I was so excited about the offer that Vangie didn't dare throw shade on my certitude that we were going to move to what I viewed as being *power plant heaven.*

She quickly acquiesced, probably because she knew it wouldn't do any good for her to fight it. I had already mentally packed and made the cross-country move. My spirit was just waiting for my body to catch up.

Vangie's only admonishment was that if we stayed in Vernal, our daughters would most likely marry Mormon boys. She simply and pointedly asked if I was okay with this. I said we would deal with that when the time came to deal with it. I am not sure this was the answer she was seeking, but I was already moving forward at breakneck speed.

The very next morning, I gave my two-week resignation at EP. They seemed genuinely surprised, but I told them I would be recommending them to do training, system descriptions, and operating procedures at the Bonanza Plant. This seemed to smooth things over. They were strictly a money machine. If I helped them make a large sale, they were more than happy to let me go. The wheels were now irreversibly in motion.

CHAPTER 2

VERNAL, UTAH

We scheduled the moving company to pack and move the following week. Deseret was paying for everything and would store our household goods until we found a place to live. Since construction was finished at the plant and the 5,000 or so construction workers were mostly gone, Rick Heller felt we would have little problem finding a place to live. They would even pay up to $3,000.00 for a down payment to purchase a residence. They would also pay for the hotel and living expenses while we searched for a home. I do not believe they could have made this move any easier. They were careful to cover *everything*.

The drive across this vast country was beautiful but also monotonous. I could not stop thinking about Bonanza Plant and what this new job was bringing with it. As excited as I was to start work there, Vangie was still as pensive about the move as when I first announced my intentions. No matter. We were on our way westward to the area we called home. We would spend 5 days in Montrose, Colorado, visiting our parents, allowing the kids to get to know their grandparents a little better before going on to Vernal.

Unfortunately, I was wholly caught up with getting to Vernal, finding a place to live, and starting work at the plant. 20/20 hindsight reveals how much of life we waste, truly waste, by focusing on future events and not living each day for its own merits. What could have been a very refreshing, enjoyable respite with family was instead filled with intense focus and prognostication about minutia and events that were wholly out of my control.

I cannot help but think of author George Bernard Shaw, who famously declared that "youth is wasted on the young." While I was no longer physically young at 29 years old, I still had serious maturity issues.

Vernal was only about 4 hours from Montrose. It made it easy to check into the Lamplighter Inn on East Main Street in Vernal with plenty of daylight left to explore, using the Mormon geographical addressing system.

The Mormon geographical addressing system is somewhat unique in America. The address system used in most Utah towns is adapted from a longitude and latitude system using north, south, east, and west coordinates. It is easier to find 2100 North and 5400 East than to find 1880 East Smivens Street if you don't already know how to get to the street called Smivens. Nonetheless, the addressing system could still be confusing.

We used a local realtor and kept finding ourselves in the little burg of Naples on the south side of Vernal. Apparently, many of the plant's temporary engineers and construction workers vacated their properties when the plant began operating. For all practical purposes, Naples was more of an area within Vernal than it was a town unto itself, but don't tell the residents of Naples, *they would be offended*.

The Vernal and Naples economy is mainly dependent on energy and drilling. The Naples area was rife with drilling companies and other industrial businesses, but the residential areas were decent, considering the lack of zoning and residential controls.

There was a relatively new, unnamed subdivision on the southeast side of Naples. Since the plant was 38 miles south of

9

Vernal, this was about as close to the plant as you could get without living in the country. Since the zoning laws were lax or even non-existent in most of the area, it was common to see livestock, chickens, or even cars without wheels sitting on blocks in people's yards. It seemed to us that very few people had any pride in their residences... *Welcome to rural Utah!*

We purchased a home located at 709 East, 2970 South, recently vacated by a plant shift supervisor who may have quit but was most likely fired. This was how it was portrayed after I started working at the plant. His loss was my gain, or so I thought.

All the homes in the subdivision were newer, nice-looking, and spacious split-level residences. Unfortunately, they were swiftly and carelessly thrown together during the initial construction boom caused by the power plant.

Our house was one of the nicest in the subdivision, but it was nothing more than a pile of wood and sheetrock haplessly (even dangerously) thrown together. It may have been nice looking, but it was a total wreck. It was constructed on 24" centers, which means the beams and joists were 24" apart. While not entirely uncommon, it's definitely cheaper than the usual 16" centers.

How our house ever passed formal code inspections (if it ever had any) is beyond me. Being a split-level home meant you entered the front door and immediately went upstairs or downstairs. The basement, or bottom floor, was not finished but had been 'roughed-in' or framed. The upstairs was spacious and finished, but everywhere you looked revealed construction deficiencies. You could clearly see the sheetrock seams throughout the house due to cracks or just plain shoddy workmanship. The paint was sloppy at best, but the code violations were nothing short of spectacular.

The upstairs main bathroom floor resembled walking on a trampoline. It *'sponged'* up and down as you walked in and it was especially noticeable if you sat on the toilet as it would drop a few inches as your bottom hit the seat. A quick glance underneath the bathroom floor (looking upwards from the unfinished basement) revealed the toilet plumbing came through the floor at the same spot a floor joist formerly crossed. The builder simply cut out two feet of floor joist with no other reinforcement. This means that the 24" centers had a 48" span that was completely unsupported under the bathroom. This, combined with cheap, thin plywood for the floor, was a recipe for disaster. It's a good thing there are not heavy things in bathrooms such as toilets, sinks, and potentially full bathtubs.

Frankly, I am certain a 300-pound or heavier person carelessly plopping down too hard on the upstairs toilet would have broken the rickety bathroom floor and dropped them, toilet and all, into the basement. Again, *welcome to rural Utah!*

There was a sliding glass door off the kitchen onto the elevated, wooden rear deck. The door was so far out of plumb that it would not fully close or lock. The supports for the wooden deck consisted of two vertical 2 x 4s nailed together on each side without the benefit of cross-bracing.

Walking on the deck caused it to sway precipitously. Any visible plumbing appeared to have been completed by a sight-impaired, drug-addled, first-year apprentice with very little formal training. The electrical was probably just as bad. With all of this in mind, what did we do? ***We purchased the house!***

Why did we buy it? It was cheap, empty, and available, and with Deseret's down payment program, we could be in it immediately. I figured I could slog through the construction deficiencies and bring the house to a safe place after we moved in. Besides, after being shoehorned into the duplex in Columbia, this house seemed like a mansion.

Unlike Delta Utah, Vernal had other churches besides Mormon Churches. One of them was Vernal Assembly of God. A portly young man named Stan Arias was the Pastor. He was about my age, maybe a year or two older, and was shaped like a squat potbelly stove. He was short and quite overweight.

Pastor Arias's wife was a pretty girl named Karen, and they had three kids. Benjamin, Hillary, and Melissa. They were a beautiful family. We immediately started Church there. Stan Arias had recently changed the name of the church from Vernal Assembly of God to World Vision Assembly of God.

Stan and Karen were giving, loving, and caring Pastors. The Church was small enough and poor enough that Karen had to work as a checker at one of the local grocery stores. She always had a smile on her face and seemed to be a hard worker and loving mother to their children.

Stan loved the Lord and absolutely lived to tell others about it. He was a natural-born Pastor and appeared willing to do anything for anyone in need. I never saw nor imagined the trouble I would end up causing this family. To this day, I am deeply and truly ashamed of my eventual actions in this Church. These were actions that had a profound and life-changing effect on my family and their family.

Overall, Vernal was not a bad of a place. It prospered *and* suffered through the building boom of the power plant but was highly experienced with boom/bust cycles due to the gas and oil energy sectors that largely supported the entire region.

On the northern outskirts of Vernal on Highway 191 was Steinaker Reservoir. It was a clean, clear lake situated in a scenic area and was the perfect size for general boating, water skiing, fishing, and family fun. About 10 miles further north was Red Fleet Reservoir. It was about the same size as Steinaker and was also a boater's paradise. If you continued about 25 more miles up the steep and winding Highway 191 into the Unitah Mountains, you would arrive at the breathtaking Flaming Gorge Reservoir.

Rising 502 feet above bedrock, Flaming Gorge Dam impounds waters of the Green River to form the Flaming Gorge reservoir extending over 90 miles into Wyoming. It has a (full) surface area of 42,020 acres. Petroglyphs (rock art) and other artifacts reveal that Fremont Indians hunted game near Flaming Gorge for many centuries.

From a boat, you could easily see up to 30' or 40' downward in the crystal-clear, bluish-green waters. The 6000-foot or so elevation of the reservoir kept it cold but still usable in the summer.

John Wesley Powell and several other men bravely rafted the Green River in crude wooden watercraft in the late 1860s. It was on May 26, 1869, that Major Powell appropriately penned the name *"Flaming Gorge"* after he and his men saw the sun radiating off the rugged, crimson cliffs. It is truly a remarkable and unforgettable region.

Vernal was a town and an area where we could have spent the rest of our lives retiring in comfort. Unfortunately, pride cometh before a fall. Make no mistake about it: *I fell extremely hard.*

CHAPTER 3

BONANZA PLANT

On my first day at the plant, I met Bill Kinsler, the plant's human resource manager. He was an interesting soul. Universally mocked within the plant, he did not display even close to an average amount of mental fortitude.

The consensus in the plant was that he was a good Mormon boy and that someone in the Deseret food chain owed a favor. The crude ones simply said he must have pictures of someone in a compromising situation, and his job was payout to keep quiet. Whatever the situation, he was a decent sort of guy who seemed marginally able to dress himself.

After receiving a recap of my benefits, Bill took me to my new office. The admin building at the Bonanza Plant was very nice, and my office was no exception. He then led me to Bob Culligan's office. Bob invited me in and asked me to take a seat.

He greeted me warmly. "Welcome aboard! I want you to take a few days to just digest this facility." He lowered his head slightly and peered out of his amply thick bifocals. "When you feel you have a good grasp of this plant, I want you to come and talk to me." He stood and held out his right hand. His grip was mediocre, and his hands were cold, but he warmly stated, "Again, welcome aboard." He then lowered his voice and, with a malevolent smile, said, "I hope this works for both of us."

This should have been a clue that something was amiss, but it would take many months for me to realize what was happening as my own pride and ambition blinded me. I thanked him for hiring me and went back to marvel at my window office, which looked onto the back of the plant and scrubber area.

The next couple of days, I was all over the plant. It was an extremely nice facility. It had a Foster Wheeler boiler and a Westinghouse turbine and generator. It used two 100% capacity steam-driven boiler feed pumps. Seeing this much excess capacity was unique, but the entire plant appeared well-engineered and rife with backup equipment.

The plant also had a baghouse and state-of-the-art wet scrubber. It was a clean-running, well-constructed plant, as near as I could tell. Unfortunately, it was not running worth a darn. It had only been in service a few months and was going through a rough shakedown period.

The plant was tripping and restarting two to five or more times a week. This was unsustainable. It makes it almost impossible to sell the power due to its undependable nature, and the trips and restarts are very hard on the plant equipment and operators.

On my first day of plant familiarization, I ventured up to the control room. As with the rest of the plant, it was a very nice control room and well insulated from the constant din of the plant equipment. Guess who I ran into? Drum roll, please...

Dan Coleman! Remember the man I detested so badly at the Holcomb Station? I bought his house in Garden City when I returned there from Delta, Utah. He was the one that, during a shift change at Holcomb Plant, irritated me so badly that I phoned this plant pretending to be him and inadvertently found this job for him.

I was taken aback when I first saw him in the Shift Supervisor's office. I knew he worked here but never considered meeting him head-on this early in my tenure at the plant. After seeing me in the control room, he jumped up from his desk, ran out of his office, and shook my right hand like I was his long-lost brother!

"Mark, how the heck are you!" He seemed genuinely pleased to see me, though I knew it had to be disingenuous because we *NEVER* liked each other at Holcomb Plant, and never bothered to pretend that we did.

"Good, Dan. How do you like it here?" I asked, not certain I wanted to hear his answer.

"Damn, this place is 1000 times better than Holcomb!" His voice dropped lower, and he looked intensely into my eyes. "The best thing you ever did for me was calling Stan, pretending to me and setting this into motion. My family and I absolutely love it here."

"I am really glad to hear this, Dan." I figured I had to say something to justify my presence here, so I continued by saying, "I wasn't sure whether this was the place to be or not, but I was sick of all the travel with Engineering Physics, and this plant was about as near to Colorado as I could probably get..." I took a breath. "Anyway, here we are."

"You're going to love it here! This is a great company to work for. They aren't cheap like Sunflower." He pointed into the Shift Supervisor's office at a couple of guys sitting in chairs by the Shift Supervisor's desk. "Do you realize that I have *TWO* Assistant Shift Supervisors to help keep this place running?"

"I heard there was a large staff," I answered flatly, looking at the two obviously bored gentlemen in his office.

"It isn't large, it is perfect. Every plant should be manned like this." He seemed jubilant and pleased with himself. I wasn't sure I agreed but kept my mouth shut (for once) out of courtesy to him.

"Cool!" I said compliantly. "I have to continue my plant familiarization process... Okay, if I roam the plant?" My asking to roam the plant was a courtesy only, as I didn't give a darn what he said. We were peer-level supervisors, and I was on a mission to learn the plant.

"That's fine. Call the control room if you're going to open any boiler doors. I don't want you getting hurt or burned." He was being condescending. I didn't need him to dictate when I could do a fire check in the furnace.

"Sure thing!" I answered with false enthusiasm, trying to cover my continuing disdain for him. I immediately left the control room.

It was abundantly apparent that this plant had a sizable staff. Everywhere you looked were operators, mechanical maintenance personnel, electricians, and instrument techs. It seemed they were staffed large enough to easily run two or three units and not just one. The office and warehouse staff also appeared to be much larger than necessary. There was certainly no shortage of workers at this plant.

During my quest to learn the plant, I visited the offices of Scott Kolar and Larry Levine. They each had large, non-window offices in the breezeway between the administration building and the plant.

I met Scott first. He was a Mormon boy in his late 30s or early 40s and was 'born and raised.' in the Utah Power and Light system. There were ample pictures of his sizable family across the front of his desk, and his office was neat and tidy to a fault... *Doesn't this guy ever do any work?*

"Hi! I am Mark Gregg. I was just hired as a Shift Supervisor." He slowly stood up from his desk and pensively shook my hand.

With undisguised revulsion, he haltingly growled, "I'm Scott Kolar." He paused, apparently for effect. "I'm the Training Manager at this plant. I heard they hired you from Engineering Physics Corporation." He glared at me for a moment. "I didn't know we were short a shift supervisor. Whose job are you taking?" His demeanor was somber and suspicious.

"They hired me as a dayshift shift supervisor. I don't know that I am replacing anyone." I was being honest with him.

"Make no mistake about it. You will be replacing someone. Our new plant manager has a nasty reputation and a plan. We just don't know what the plan is right now." He was not hiding his animus for Bob Culligan, nor did he want to spend any time with me.

"Let me take you next door to meet Larry Levine. He can provide you with prints and plant information so you can start learning about this plant." He stood up, lumbering past me to the door. We stepped to the office next door to his. It was a similar but slightly smaller office.

19

"Larry, this is Mark Gregg. He is the new dayshift shift supervisor." His voice was riddled with skepticism. Larry was in his forties, lean, reeked of cigarette smoke, and wore oversized horn-rim glasses. He looked as if he had not shaved in a few days. His office lacked the tidiness of Scott's office. Larry stood and very aggressively shook my hand.

"How ya doin?" His voice was deep and had an odd southern twang to it.

"I'm doing well, thanks! Scott said you had prints and other information to aid me in learning a little about this plant." I tried to be as upbeat as possible.

"Ya came to the right place, man." He said slowly as he began rummaging through a pile of prints and other information on a cluttered side table in his office. "I got all the goods right here." After pulling out some 11" x 17" prints and some other documentation, he turned to me and coyly said, "Day shift, shift supervisor, huh? Odd, I surely don't know why we need one of them. I think there is more going on here than just hiring a shift supervisor." He looked at me suspiciously. "You came from Engineering Physics, right?"

"I did," I answered, trying to stay upbeat and positive. "I am originally from Western Colorado but have worked at several different plants like Bridger and Four Corners. I even worked at Holcomb Plant in western Kansas with Dan Coleman."

He gave a half-hearted laugh. "Sorry to hear that!" I laughed when he said it. I wasn't sure if he was denigrating the Holcomb Plant, Dan Coleman, or both.

"I know, right?" I answered quickly. The three of us all laughed. This was the first time Scott showed any emotion other than repressed anger and suspicion.

Larry continued in his faint, odd southern drawl. "Well, sir, I have been all over this industry and started up a ton of plants." He puffed up like a bullfrog and began detailing his long and impressive pedigree. He appeared to have been all around the industry and was quite proud of it.

Scott interrupted him, probably because he heard Larry's crap-spiel many times previously.

"I have work to do. If you need anything else, let us know." Scott seemed to have a chip on his shoulder. I didn't know if it was me or a bad day. He left Larry's office, allowing the large, heavy steel door to slam closed behind him.

"How well do you know our new leader?" Larry asked suspiciously after the door slammed closed.

"I don't know him personally. I just met him during the interview a few weeks ago."

Larry studied me skeptically for a moment. "Hmmm. It just don't add up." He seemed concerned.

"What doesn't add up?" I asked, trying to figure out what he was talking about.

"Why they hired another shift supervisor when we have too many already. I'll tell ya, that son-of-a-bitch has made it clear he thinks the plant is f!@%$ over-staffed." He was openly cynical and angry now.

"I don't have a clue. I was hired into this plant after being told I was a day shift shift supervisor." I was sincere because it was the truth.

Larry continued. "Believe me, someone is going to get screwed on this deal. I can see it coming from a mile away. They will be sorely screwed! I just don't know who it will be." He was shaking his head, and his demeanor had turned openly nasty.

"If I hear anything, I will let you know." I was trying to connect with him on some level so he didn't view me as the enemy. To help reinforce this, I said, "In fact, if you hear anything, let me know. Right now, I am in the dark on this whole deal."

We talked for a few more minutes. He emphasized his importance to the plant because he was one of the few people here who *"truly understood power plants."* He told me this to justify why he was in the training department. The more he talked, the less impressed I was. I am certain he had a tremendous amount of experience. It was certainly more than I had. However, he appeared to be extremely insecure.

I spent another few days walking through the plant and reading everything available. The wet scrubber had a substantial number of systems I had never worked with. One of them was a huge, rotating, screened vacuum drum to dewater the scrubber sludge. It was fascinating to watch as it continuously peeled off a gelatinous layer of what resembled sheet rock without its paper backing. It would crumble in the chute and fall onto a conveyor, which would take it to the plant waste disposal area. As with all the other areas of the plant, the scrubber and coal handling areas appeared to be drowning with excess personnel.

The prints that Larry Levine gave me were, of course, developed by Burns and McDonnell, the company that designed the plant. However, the written system descriptions and operating procedures were written by the plant training department... *Scott and Larry*. The information in them appeared to be sound, but the grammar, presentation, and sentence structure were all horrendously bad. However, the technical content seemed somewhat valid, as far as I could tell.

Several days later, when I was comfortable with my overall knowledge of the plant, I stopped by Bob Culligan's office to see when he would like to meet. He immediately invited me into his office.

"What do you think of this facility now that you have had a detailed look?" He wasted no time jumping into my thoughts about the plant.

"Overall, it appears to be a well-engineered plant." I wasn't sure what he was looking for, so I decided to let him carry the conversation.

"Yes, yes, it is." His eyes narrowed, and his expression turned ominous. "Unfortunately, they are not keeping it running. Our operational track record is abysmal and isn't improving." He paused and slowly dropped his head to peer over his glasses. His voice lowered to a barely discernable mumble. "Son, are you Mormon?"

I was totally shocked at this inappropriate and instantaneous change of subject that dropped out of nowhere. Completely caught off-guard, I answered cautiously. "No sir, I am not."

"I was hoping that was the case." He smiled tightly, leaned back into his chair, and casually locked his hands behind the back of his head. "Frankly, I hired you because I need your help to clean up this mess and get this plant running as it should." He then put his arms back on the desk and leaned forward, peering over the top of his glasses again. "As you pointed out, it's a nice plant, but it certainly isn't running like a nice plant." His voice, again, lowered to barely a growl. "We have to reduce the manning in this plant *way below* 100 people." He emphasized the *"way below"* part.

I was overwhelmed with everything just thrown at me. Trying to cover my surprise and look at least partially intelligent, I asked, "What is the current number of employees on this plant site right now?"

"The boneheads at Deseret headquarters in Sandy allowed the staffing to reach 147 people. Of course, they were staffing for what they thought was going to be two units and not just one." I already knew the Deseret headquarters was in a suburb of Salt Lake City called Sandy.

Trying to ensure he knew I was onboard with everything he said, I sycophantically stated, "I have definitely noticed that there are *waaaay* too many people for a plant of this size." I then paused and asked, "So there is definitely going to be only one unit here?"

"Yes, and from the confidential reports I have read, they probably should not have built this unit. Someone at Deseret headquarters was apparently trying to build an empire. Frankly, I have not met one of those people in Sandy who has impressed me in the least. They appear to be a bunch of ignorant, inbred bastards."

Once again, I was completely astonished at his blunt and candid assessment of his superiors. Deep in the back of my mind, I knew he had a reputation for cleaning up the plants he managed. I was just blindsided and, on several (very) dark levels, thrilled by the notion that he appeared to want me as a part of his 'inside' group.

He then pointedly asked me something that made a shiver run down my spine. "I noticed on your resume that you spent a very short time at Intermountain Power Plant in Delta, Utah... Why is that?" Before I could even answer, he jumped back in. "I wanted to ask you this during your interview, but Stan was there, and I didn't want to compromise you if your answer was what I thought it would be."

"Well, to be honest, we were struggling with being outsiders." I felt intensely two-faced with this explanation because the situation at Intermountain was far more complex than I could easily explain at this moment. One thing's for certain: I did not want to admit that the whole situation at Intermountain was my fault and not theirs.

I didn't know it then, but in the coming months, I would quickly outgrow any feelings of being two-faced, duplicitous, or hypocritical. The longer Bob and I worked together, the easier it became to justify my actions, right or wrong.

As I answered, he slowly nodded his head in agreement. "Just exactly what I figured." His demeanor relaxed as he continued. "Are you on board with helping me clean up this plant?"

"Absolutely, I think I would enjoy being a part of a quest for plant improvement." I could not see just how much I was puffing up with abject pride and self-righteousness. Unfortunately, it was just beginning.

We talked for another thirty minutes or more about our families and our previous backgrounds when he abruptly changed the subject, reached into his desk, and said, "Edit these documents and bring them back to me as soon as you are finished." I glanced at them and saw I had already read several of them.

"I will get these back to you as soon as possible. Thanks for the time and insight into the situation here. I will do my best to help in any way I can." I was sincerely upbeat and excited to do this for him. My intentions at this point were honorable. I honestly wanted to help.

He then, again, peered over the top of his glasses and stated with extreme intensity, "Everything we discussed here is confidential. It would be quite upsetting to me if *anything* we discussed left this room."

A chill again slid down my spine. One look in his eyes made me realize just how serious he was. With little contemplation, I answered very sincerely, "Not a word... Thanks for trusting me."

It took several hours to edit the horrendously bad documents he supplied. I had already read most of them, trying to glean information about the plant. As I had observed, they were very poorly written documents.

When someone writes: ***"The spinning rotor of the turbine is directly connected to the spinning rotor of the generator by a coupling that is spinning in a correspondingly identical rotational direction that is counter to a clock if observed from the end of the generator where the exciter is located."*** It appears to me they are trying to make themselves

26

look intelligent when, in fact, it revealed EXTREME ignorance of grammar and sentence structure.

The obvious way to write this would be: ***"The turbine and generator are coupled together and spin counter-clockwise looking from the generator end."*** It is simple, straight forward, and much easier to understand.

There were statements such as, ***"do not, not monitor this when the plant is running as it could have problems that not monitoring it would cause you to not see."*** Really? *Are you kidding me?*

How about writing it this way? ***"When the plant is operating, this must be monitored on a regular basis."***

By the time I completed the few documents Bob provided, they appeared to be bleeding to death. Using a red pen to edit them, I would slash out whole paragraphs and condense them down to one sentence. I filled the margins and back of each page with comments, critiques, and entire rewrites. Oddly, I had very few comments on data accuracy; they were primarily about grammar, sentence structure, spelling, and word usage.

When I completed the edits, I went to Bob's office and stuck my head into his door, "I have the edits you asked for on those system description documents. Let me know when you would like to see them."

He immediately jumped up from his desk, "Please, bring them in now!" while motioning me into his office. I walked to his large desk and handed them to him. "Have a seat." He then quickly paged through the messy, nearly crimson documents. His intensity seemed to ramp steadily upward as he moved from page to page. I felt like I was a trick pony waiting for my next command. I didn't enjoy sitting and watching him thumb through the pages.

My restlessness got the best of me. I couldn't handle sitting there any longer. I hesitantly said, "I can come back and discuss these with you when you are ready." He never looked up, as he curtly replied, "Just sit there." He continued to riffle through the documents.

Several more excruciatingly long minutes passed. He then looked up with a sinister smile and proclaimed, "This is precisely what I need." He slapped the documents down on his desk. "How would you feel about rewriting the training material at this plant?" Somehow, I felt I was not going to have a choice. It was, finally, completely clear to me why I was hired.

"No problem!" I confidently replied. I honestly didn't mind doing the system descriptions and operating procedures. I was quite experienced after my time in Engineering Physics.

He sat back in his chair and locked his hands behind his head. This was becoming a defining look for him when he was satisfied with himself. "Why don't you continue plant familiarization and let me work with these documents." I left the office and ventured into the plant, ruminating about what he meant by his statement that he wanted to "work with these documents."

The next morning, I arrived at the plant, grabbed a cup of coffee, and was sitting in my office looking over the large pile of training materials that I would likely be rewriting during the coming months. About an hour later, I saw Larry Levine walking through the admin building, carrying a large box in front of him. He appeared to be escorted by one of the security guards who were normally at the front gate.

I walked over to Bob's office, but he wasn't there. Carlene Crane, the executive secretary, was in her office. As I stepped in, I noticed her eyes were red. She was crying. I gently asked, "Is something wrong?" She immediately turned, grabbed a tissue, and dabbed her eyes.

"Bob is firing Scott and Larry." She sniffled and looked away. I didn't know her well enough to try and console her. Besides, I was blown away at how quickly this occurred. I immediately felt blamed for it.

I went back to my office. About 15 minutes later Scott Kolar exited the office with a heavily loaded box. He looked extremely pissed, and his face was flushed crimson. The security guard was also carrying a box. Scott obviously had many more personal items in his office than Larry. I felt significant dread as I recalled the pictures of Scott's large family on his desk.

It was only a few minutes later when my desk phone rang. It was Bob. He tersely commanded me, "come to my office. I need to talk to you now." I immediately walked over to his office.

"Close the door and take a seat." He seemed stoic and indifferent as I entered his office and sat down. "I fired Scott and Larry this morning." He looked me straight in the eyes as he said this, probably to gauge my response.

"I saw them being escorted out," I answered carefully as I sat unwavering, even though I felt a high degree of responsibility.

"Do you want to hear something sad?" he asked impatiently. "Those two bastards have spent hundreds of thousands of dollars of Deseret's money and have not trained a soul. They have sat up there for over two damn years playing with themselves and producing crappy, unusable documents in the name of training." He took on an air of disgust. "It is inexcusable that it took so long to correct the situation."

I wasn't sure what to say. I just stared at him, trying to show as little emotion as possible. I didn't have to wait long. He jumped directly into his reason for calling me into his office.

"I want you to move from your office into Scott's. You can also have full access to Larry's office. I want the training materials rewritten, and I want something else." There was a pregnant pause.

"What's that?" I asked, not sure I wanted to hear the answer.

"I want a maintenance apprenticeship developed for this plant. I want a state-sanctioned apprenticeship for the maintenance, electrical, and instrumentation personnel so they can earn their money through competency steps. Do you think you can set this up?"

"I've never done anything like that before, but I am certain I can make it happen." I tried to project an air of confidence. However, I was reeling in self-doubt and guilt and overwhelmed at how much was just dumped on me.

"I want a game plan on my desk detailing your steps to complete the training material re-writes and your approach to putting an apprenticeship in place by next Monday morning." He stared directly at me with a Mona Lisa smile.

30

"One more thing…" He paused for effect. "You are now the Bonanza Plant Training and Technical Support Superintendent. As a superintendent, you will attend the morning meetings with the other superintendents, carry a pager, and participate in the shared weekend duties." His eyes narrowed. "In six months, we will see how effective you have been and will adjust your salary accordingly. Does this work for you?"

By now, my face was numb, and I was overwhelmed to the point of apoplexy. It took me several moments to gather my composure. "Yes sir, it sounds good. I will do my best to not let you down."

In a few moments, I went from a Shift Supervisor to a Superintendent level with more on my plate than what seemed humanly possible to achieve in a year's time. It was obvious that I was set up to be a key player in his quest to "clean up this plant."

We talked for another 20 or so minutes. During that time, he spoke quite disparagingly of Stan Gorman and most of the shift supervisors. The only shift supervisor he had high praise for was Don Pillar, my old nemesis and eventual buddy from Bridger and LRS. This bolstered my confidence in his ability to evaluate people. Don had his flaws, but he was, by far, the best powerhouse guy I had ever known.

It was now obvious there was going to be a blood bath at the plant. He needed to reduce the manpower and was bound and determined to eliminate those he considered the least competent as soon as possible. What's worse, I had the distinct impression that being a Mormon had a high degree of landing you in the incompetent category…

31

CHAPTER 4

RECREATIONAL WONDERLAND!

Life away from the Bonanza Plant was initially enjoyable. The recreational wonderland that surrounded Vernal demanded that we participate! We purchased (or traded for) three different boats while in Vernal. I knew we needed a boat because of the proximity of beautiful lakes (Steinaker, Red Fleet, and Flaming Gorge). The first one came from Ralph Aranda, my brother-in-law.

Vangie's sister Alice married a gargantuan fellow named Ralph Aranda when she was in her late teens. Ralph was a consummately rough around the edges redneck. Okay… Forget the edges, he was rough to the core. Though not scholastically inclined, he was very mechanical, a hard worker, and could do anything he put his mind to.

Ralph was a grizzly bear of a man, big in every way, with large mutton-chop sideburns containing more hair than most men had on their heads. Some people thought he had a mean streak in him. Frankly, I never had a problem with Ralph. In fact, he defended me on more than one occasion.

Vangie's sister Linda married a 'Super-Mex' named Lawrence Barajas. Lawrence had issues with whites and their treatment of Hispanics. He was a prolific drinker and was a mean and obnoxious drunk. He and Linda divorced not too many years after being married.

Because of his overt dislike of "gringos," Vangie and I were not around Lawrence other than family dinner outings. During big family get-togethers, he would drink heavily and then diligently try to pick a fight with me or at least make me look like a coward. Ralph would not have any of it. On several occasions, Ralph 'gently' stepped in. Ralph's best and final intervention happened during one of our visits to Montrose when Vangie's parents threw a big dinner for everyone. His intervention was less than gentle this time.

Lawrence, as always, was thoroughly liquored up. Without warning, after dinner, he put his face into mine and ripped into me with a scorching diatribe in Spanish. I didn't have a clue what he even said, though I did identify several Spanish expletives.

With instantaneous surprise to everyone, Ralph jumped-up, violently wrapping his muscular arm around the gaunt and spindly Lawrence, swooping him up like a limp and floppy rag doll. The air instantly purged from Lawrence's lungs in a painfully visceral *"OOOMPH"* as his scrawny body slammed forcefully against the side of the house.

Ralph compressed him firmly against the wall in a virtual death   grip. He allowed the total shock to penetrate Lawrence's pickled brain before growling directly into his now completely ashen face.

"Pendejo, you ever touch my buddy again, I will @&%!$ end you." He paused once more, staring directly into Lawrence's horror-stricken eyes. "You got me, *pendajo*?"

I don't recall Lawrence ever answering. You could hear a pin drop in the previously chaotic backyard as everyone simultaneously inhaled, waiting for Ralph to send small chunks of Lawrence's mangled cadaver all over the backyard. Instead, Ralph ceased his death grip just as quickly as he grabbed him.

Lawrence staggered precariously as he came off the wall. Ralph immediately turned to me like nothing ever happened and cheerfully said, "You gotta come and see my boat. I just re-upholstered the seats, and it looks great!"

Lawrence never gave me another disparaging look. From that day on, he acted like we were the best of friends despite the fact that we never talked or even looked at each other. Pretty certain Ralph wasn't kidding and even more confident that Lawrence knew this.

Later that day, we went to Ralph and Alice's house and looked at his boat. His boat was an old fiberglass 16' V-hull boat with a closed bow. Old is the operative word. However, he put a modern 70 HP Johnson outboard motor on it and reupholstered the seats himself with sparkly red, marine vinyl.

Ralph was very handy at anything he put his mind to. The seats didn't look half bad. Turned out he was selling it. Who knew? I bought it on the spot because it was in our price range (cheap), and he was currently my hero. *I still think Ralph was way smarter than he ever let on.*

We began using the boat almost immediately. Being that I was on straight days at the plant, I would come home from work, and Vangie would already have the boat loaded and a picnic lunch prepared. We would drive the twenty-minute drive to Steinaker and spend the rest of the evening in the water. We purchased skis, toys, fishing poles, and fishing tackle. We learned the art of trolling for trout and always caught a mess of fish. We cherished this time with each other and loved eating fresh trout.

Vangie grew up water skiing and taught the kids and me to water ski. She was an excellent skier, and I enjoyed pulling her behind our under-powered, aging V-hull boat. In fact, the 70-horsepower Johnson outboard contributed to me almost killing Vangie.

It did not take long to realize that a heavy fiberglass boat, a family of five, their gear, and a 5,500-foot elevation with only 70 horsepower was not a good mix. *We needed more power*. I found a boat dealer in Grand Junction, Colorado, that took my 70 HP Johnson outboard motor in-trade with some cash to purchase an older Evinrude 115 HP motor. It may have been an older unit, but it ran great.

We marveled at the amazing performance increase on our first outing to Steinaker Lake with the new outboard motor. Without struggling, Vangie could now pop out of the water like a cork. I pulled her around the lake as the kids cheered her on (as they always did). She would jump the wake and always put on a show for them. They loved it. I loved her.

As always, I pulled Vangie back around by the swimming area, staying well out of the wakeless zone. I then banked the wheel on the boat while applying full throttle. The boat rapidly whipped her across the wake and into the shore. I would then circle around and drop down to a few miles an hour (wakeless speed) to beach the boat.

As I banked the boat and applied full throttle, I never considered that I had 40% more power than the old 70 HP outboard. The boat enthusiastically responded to full throttle by accelerating rapidly, whipping Vangie across the wake about twice as fast as ever before. As soon as she let go of the rope, we both instantly realized just how fast she was going… Straight for the shore with kids playing in the water and on the beach.

She skillfully avoided any swimmers while slamming into the beach at breakneck speed. I saw her try and jump from the skis as they stuck into the sand. It resembled a slow-motion plane wreck sans the flames and fire. She flew into the air, arms, and legs outstretched and flailing. There were at least two 'touch and goes' before she came to a rest on her back. I looked at Brandi... Her eyes were bulging as she watched her mother slam into the beach.

"I think I just killed your mama!" I exclaimed as I placed the boat into neutral. 20/20 hindsight... This was probably not the best thing to tell a 10-year-old girl about her mother. Once again, *who knew?*

We pulled into shore, beaching the boat. Vangie was still lying on her back. The kids and I ran over and found her in extreme pain. We sat there for several more minutes before she slowly, painfully arose and resumed living. Unfortunately, she has dealt with serious problems with her neck and upper back ever since.

A few years later, an X-ray revealed that she sustained a fracture of her collarbone. Wow! I wasn't even trying to kill her. We had several other mishaps with this boat that we still look back on with fondness.

One of them happened about a month later. We were at the lake for several hours. It was now dusk, but I wanted to go for one more spin around the lake on water skis. We were on the edge of the wakeless zone. I was in the water, and the boat was at the other end of the rope, further away from the shore. An aging, gnarly Park Ranger was on the beach by the swimming area and hollered something. I couldn't make out what he said but assumed he was telling us to move further away from the wakeless area. Okay, no problem...

I motioned for Vangie to pull me further out from the wakeless area before applying power. Once we repositioned, I hollered at her to "HIT IT!" This was always our signal to pour the power to the boat. I came up on both skis and had a good ski all the way around the lake. As we came around by the boat ramp, the Park Ranger appeared, angrily flailing his arms and yelling at us from the pier. Vangie dropped the boat from Warp Drive, and I entered the water. She circled, picked me up, and we wakelessly pulled to the pier.

Wow! Was that curmudgeonly Park Ranger angry! He had apparently hollered, *"It is too dark to continue water skiing. Get out of the water!"* What did we do? We openly defied him and in front of God and everyone on the beach, we put the power to the boat and went water skiing. We tried to explain that we didn't hear what he said, but he wasn't in the mood to listen to *anything* we had to say.

In 1986, Vangie received a $150.00 citation for failing to obey an officer of the law and pulling a skier after dark. She wasn't very happy with me. Please understand that I honestly never heard what he was yelling at us from the shore. Neither the Ranger nor Vangie found any humor in the incident. I still occasionally laugh about it (to myself). This certainly wasn't the end of our boating adventures or misadventures.

There was an old, faded, turquoise tri-hull boat with an open bow sitting in the yard of a decrepit double-wide mobile home on the outskirts of Vernal. I drove by it every day on the way to work. The outboard motor was a Chrysler, but the engine cover was missing, and age and the elements appeared to have taken their toll on what was left. It caught my fancy because it was an open-bow boat. We didn't know it at the time we bought Ralph's boat, but without an open bow, there is very little room in a 16' boat for a family of five and their fishing poles and/or water skis.

I stopped at the aging double-wide trailer after work one day. An older couple that seemed to not mind living in squalor answered the door. I asked if they were interested in selling the faded turquoise boat in their yard. The old man's reply was not unexpected.

He grunted, "I plan to fix that boat and put 'er back in the water someday."

I am certain this was code words for, "I am a hopelessly lost hoarder, and that boat is one of my many possessions that will rot away in the very spot it is sitting." Indeed, the seats were rotted, the boat was severely sun-bleached, and the engine was a total loss. The trailer was seriously rusted and had two flat tires. It had been sitting for quite some time.

I thanked him for his time and left. However, I couldn't get that boat out of my mind.

Several days later, I saw an ad on a gas station bulletin board as I filled my car with gas. It was sloppily hand-written and said:

1950's Evinrude 5 HP Motor. Old, but runs good. $75.00 or best offer.

I drove straight from the gas station to an old farmhouse east of Vernal. The engine was, indeed, old. It looked more valuable as an antique in a museum than a usable engine. It was sitting in a barrel of filthy, oil-fouled water. The old farmer yanked on the starter rope 10 or 11 times before it reluctantly started. After warming up, it seemed to run well. I offered him $50.00. We settled on $60.00. I now owned an ancient, museum-grade, Evinrude outboard motor.

On a complete hunch, I borrowed a portable engine hoist and, with much difficulty, removed the 115 HP Evinrude and all the control and steering cables from the back of our boat. The new motor was only 5 horsepower, and it took little effort to install it in place of the big engine. I did not attach the steering cable or controls because the new motor was controlled locally from an attached lever. I then unbolted and removed all the seats from the boat.

I drove back to the double-wide where the open-bow boat I inquired about earlier was sitting and, again, knocked on the door. The old man barely cracked the door. Upon seeing me, he slowly opened it and gave me a suspicious look, saying, "What chu want?"

"I have a proposition for you." I was trying to be as upbeat as possible. I needed this to work because if it didn't, I just did a ton of work for nothing, plus I would have to put everything back on my boat to make it usable again.

"What chu got?" He growled skeptically.

"I will give you a nice, running boat on a nice trailer for your old tri-hull." I turned and pointed to the boat behind my pick-up. "Come out and take a look at it."

He turned back into the house and hollered, "Ma, you ought to come see what this boy's got." An aging, disheveled woman emerged from their hovel, looking very apprehensive. The two of them slowly walked out to my boat.

I directed them to the back of the boat. "The engine runs well. I will start it for you, but I can't let it run for more than a few moments, or it will overheat because it is not in the water."

"Where's the seats?" The old man looked perturbed.

"Unfortunately, there isn't any, but I will unbolt and move the seats from your boat and put them into this one as a part of the deal." I gave them some time to walk around the boat. Eager to make the trade, I pushed as hard as I could. "My trailer is in great shape, much better shape than yours. The lights all work, and the wheel bearings were recently packed."

I could see that I had piqued their interest, or at least his. She seemed entirely aloof and disinterested. I decided now was the time to take the kill shot. "The engine is too small to water ski behind, but you could be fishing in this boat tomorrow if you wanted to trade me straight across for your old tri-hull."

Raising his head slightly, he looked at the old woman and coyly grunted, "What chu think, woman?"

She turned and slowly started towards the front door of the house as she murmured, "Do what you want… You always do."

The old man asked me to start the engine. I had put a new spark plug in it and cleaned the gas tank of the smelly, old, varnished fuel that had probably been in it for years. It now started and ran like a new engine. When I shut it back off, he looked at me while lethargically rubbing his chin and said, "Sounds good, but she's an old motor." I knew I had to act quickly.

"Tell you what, I will throw in $20.00 for your first fishing trip. I can have your seats in it by tomorrow afternoon."

The old man looked directly at me with a barely discernible smile. "You got yourself a deal."

I was elated. I took our boat home and then went after the tri-hull. I had to change the tires to get it home. After doing so, I swapped the sun-rotted, mouse-infested seats from the tri-hull to our old boat and took it back to the old man, giving him the highly anticipated $20.00. I also had him sign a bill of sale.

In the coming days, Vangie worked her fingers to the bone, tearing out the remnants of sun-rotted indoor/outdoor carpeting and replacing it with new marine carpeting. She painstakingly scrubbed, polished, and waxed the deeply clouded and fading turquoise fiberglass over and over until it shined like a new boat. We installed the sparkly red marine vinyl seats from the old boat and then mounted and connected the 115 HP Evinrude motor to the back. I packed the wheel bearings and put new tires on the trailer. When finished with all this, the old turquoise, tri-hull, open-bow boat looked pretty darn nice!

We used it several times at Steinaker. It was great to have the open bow as it provided much-needed room and met our needs well. We then decided to take it up to Flaming Gorge and go camping. I purchased a used electric trolling motor and mounted it on the back. The 115 HP Evinrude was just too much engine to try and troll. You were moving too fast, even at a low idle.

We purchased a new, large tent and some air mattresses to put our sleeping bags on. After extensive preparation, we pulled the boat up the mountain to the magnificent Flaming Gorge reservoir.

We found a beautiful camping spot right on the water. We beached the boat about 30' from the tent and had everything you could ever long for on a camping trip. A massive, picturesque, clear-water reservoir, trees, nature, campfire, and the ability to catch as many cold-water trout as you could possibly eat (or so we thought).

We water skied, played in the reservoir until late in the afternoon, and then went trolling for trout. The electric trolling motor worked great, but we weren't finding the bounty of fresh trout we expected. We fired-up the Evinrude and motored to a long, deep, somewhat foreboding canyon on the Utah side of the reservoir. The water was ominously dark, and there was no beach or shoreline due to the steepness of the canyon walls.

We trolled for about two hours, pushing deeper and deeper into the continuously narrowing canyon before deciding we didn't have a clue what we were doing. We always caught tons of fish at Steinaker and heard that Flaming Gorge was even better. Unfortunately, this evening, the trout weren't buying what we were selling.

Before we knew it, we were in the deep shadows of dusk. I was a little alarmed because of the previous ticket for boating after dark. I knew we had to get back to the campsite. We drew-in our lines, lifted the electric trolling motor out of the water, and I turned the key to start the Evinrude. It made about two strained, *whump, whump,* revolutions and stopped.

Hmmm… It seemed I had run down the two car batteries that provided trolling motor power as well as starting power for the Evinrude. No problem. I could take the engine cover off and use a rope on the flywheel to start the 115 HP Evinrude outboard.

Wrapping a chunk of water-ski rope around the flywheel, I pulled with all my strength. There was another *very slow, very strained, WHUMP, WHUMP* sound as the Evinrude's pistons came to the top dead center on their compression stroke. No problem. I would just pull harder... Okay, *problem.* The compression was too much for me to start the engine. I tried until I was exhausted. Vangie and I tried together. We could not spin that engine fast enough for it to start.

The kids were now getting hungry, as we had already eaten all the snacks. The problem was the pervasive darkness that was overtaking us in the narrow canyon. It was spooky and eerily silent other than unexplained splashes of water, we presumed from fish jumping and laughing at our predicament.

We could not beach the boat due to the steep canyon walls, nor did we want to. We needed to get these kids back to the tent, feed them, and settle them down for the night. We were already completely exhausted from a full day of activities.

We grabbed the coast Guard-mandated, small plastic oar, and one water ski that was now conscripted as a second oar. We both leaned over the edges of the boat and began paddling out of that canyon. The first couple of hours weren't too bad, but by the third hour, we were getting blisters on our hands. The kids were now fast asleep, and we could not see *ANYTHING* due to the thick, consuming darkness.

When we finally reached the main channel, there were no boats or any signs of human life on the lake. We were hoping for a tow from another boater. This may have been a reality 4 or 5 hours earlier. *I am now certain I heard fish laughing hysterically below the boat.*

Vangie and I paddled that turquoise tri-hull all the way back to the campsite, arriving after midnight. It was cold, we were hungry and exhausted, and every tendon, muscle, and joint in our bodies radiated with pain.

We put the kids into bed and collapsed into our sleeping bags, clothes and all. Our next remembrance was the kids shaking us and saying, "Mommy, daddy, wake up. We're hungry, and it's time for breakfast!" Vangie and I had sore muscles for at least a week. Despite my idiocy, we thoroughly enjoyed that boat and happily finished the season with it.

In the spring of 1987, we traded the old tri-hull in on a brand new, Beachcraft 195 Cuddy. The cuddy designation is a closed bow, but it was BIG and had two small windows in the cuddy (bow) area. It had plush marine carpeting in the cuddy and was big enough to comfortably sleep two adults in sleeping bags. It was also great to store tons of gear. The engine was a fuel-injected, 175 HP Mariner Outboard.

We loved this boat and towed it all over the country as we moved again (and again and again). These were the happy times in Vernal. Unfortunately, the remainder of our tenure there became much darker and deeply complex.

CHAPTER 5

STEP INTO MY OFFICE

The pace at Bonanza Plant was intense. I was rewriting all the training material and working to build an apprenticeship for the maintenance departments. I was also in Bob Culligan's office for private meetings... *Continuously.* This, combined with being considered Superintendent level and sharing the weekend duties, began working on my head. I began to bask in a grossly inflated view of my status at the plant. It reminded me of the former Secretary of State under former President Ronald Reagan, *Alexander Haig.* In 1981, following the March 30 assassination attempt on Reagan, Haig intensely asserted before God, the World, and witnessing reporters, *"I am in control here now!"*

The video clip of an ardent, aggressive Mr. Haig was played over and over ad-nauseum by the press, presumably to discredit him. The sheer intensity of his proclamation matches my psyche in 1987 at Bonanza Plant. The more the plant personnel sensed I was a pipeline to Bob Culligan, the more sought after I became. This increased my perceived importance at a square root function to the number of people coming into my office.

During this same time period, my ego had another wholly unneeded and undeserved boost due to a major incident that occurred in the plant. My old nemesis at Holcomb Station, Dan Coleman, was on dayshift. He attended the morning meeting and reported the unit was running well. After the meeting, I went back to my office to work on documentation. A few hours later, the high-pitched howl of the steam turbine changed rapidly, and the plant paging system immediately went crazy. You could always tell something was amiss by the urgency (or panic) in the plant pages.

I immediately left my office and ventured into the plant to see what was happening. I had to climb a flight of stairs and then cross the turbine deck to get into the control room.

The control room was in a state of semi-controlled chaos, as always when a unit trips. There was the continuous blasting of the alarms, and the control operator and Dan were both standing in-front of the control boards, grasping the paging phones and looking intense.

"What happened?" I asked anxiously as I walked over to the board. I was the first management person in the control room.

Dan never looked back. He tersely answered, "The boiler tripped."

"What caused it, do you know?"

He glanced back at me with malice in his eyes and snarled, "Go back to your office, we are busy here." He couldn't have surprised me more if he had hit me with a brick. He had no right to speak to me this way. It didn't help that we always hated each other, and this was just an added insult to injury.

I held my temper and stood my ground, watching their actions. By not leaving the control room, I was intentionally escalating our on-going feud. As I studied the control board, I realized the turbine/generator was still *online*. He had lost all fires in the boiler, and instead of tripping the turbine as he was supposed to, he ran the load on the turbine/generator down to about 5 MW and was trying to do a purge on the boiler. *This is potential suicide.*

I raised my voice in alarm and blurted out, "Dan, why do you still have the generator on-line? You don't have fires in the boiler." I raised my voice. "You are flirting with water induction!"

He ominously narrowed his eyes and thrust out his right arm. His index finger pointing towards the control room door, he shrieked. "I told you to get the hell out of my control room!"

I ignored his anger and repeated my warning. "Dan, you're going to water induct the turbine!"

His face went crimson with rage as he looked at a data point on one of the data acquisition displays near him. "I still have 955° main steam temperature. Go ahead and tell me how I can water induct with this kind of temperature, Einstein!"

"You are condensing inside the pendants!" I yelled, dramatically lifting both my arms with my hands out towards him. "At 5 MW, your steam flow is so low that you lose all differential across the pendants. With no fires in the boiler, they are no longer superheaters but condensers. The pendants that still have flow are giving you false security with the high temperature. If the pendants clean out, you are screwed!"

This time, he looked at me with violence in his eyes. "You have **NO AUTHORITY** in this control room. I'm not going to tell you again, **GET THE F&@$! OUT OF MY CONTROL ROOM BEFORE I THROW YOU OUT**."

Dan had PTSD from his army time in Vietnam... He would freak out under pressure and get insanely mad and potentially violent. Judging from his current demeanor, I knew I only had a few seconds to leave, or we would be in a physical altercation... ***One that we would both ultimately lose.*** I reluctantly left the control room.

Crossing the turbine deck, I turned and went down the stairs. I was preparing to enter the admin building when I was jarred to my core by what I thought was an explosion. Everything instantaneously went dark, and debris, dust, and steam were engulfing me. I instantly dropped to a fetal position, covering my head with my arms. For a split second, I honestly thought my time on Earth was finished... I honestly believed I was going to die.

Trying to make sense of what happened, I moved my arms and legs to determine the extent of trauma to my body. It took a few moments to realize I was scared spitless but physically seemed to be unscathed. I then became acutely aware of steam blasting from the front end of the turbine. Gathering my wits about me, I started taking in the damage to the plant.

It appeared the 40+ inch diameter main steam line ripped completely off its hangars about 50' or 60' from me. When it ripped from the hangars, it dropped, smashing into the cinder block wall that separates the boiler room from the turbine room. The weight of the massive main steam line was far too much for cinder blocks, and they disintegrated and exploded from the impact. The debris from the blocks was blown over a large area. A steam/water mixture was blowing deafeningly hard from what looked like the main turbine throttle valves. It was just too dark and dusty to see clearly. I was certain there was extensive damage.

I gathered my senses as best I could and moved cautiously back up to the control room in the near darkness. A shiver ran down my spine as I crossed under the now mangled main steam line. Dan and his control room operator were both ashen and stunned, almost in a state of shock.

Dan, baffled, looked directly at me, and quietly stammered, "What the hell happened?" His demeanor had changed from abject anger to a disheveled and clueless flunky.

"You water inducted the damn turbine!" I screeched angrily as I walked over to the turbine area of the control board. It was now tripped and rolling down with extremely high vibration.

"I don't understand," he mumbled, "we had good superheat temperature..." His voice trailed off.

Stan Gorman, the Ops Superintendent, came flying into the control room and ran directly over to the board. It was only a few moments later that Bob Culligan, along with the plant Engineering Manager and many others from the front office, piled into the control room. I hung around for a bit before going out to measure the damage.

Unfortunately, the post-mortem revealed exactly what I had predicted. He severely water inducted the main turbine. The slug of water that cleaned out of the superheater pendants in the boiler caused a massive water hammer that ripped the main steam line off its hangars and then damaged the sealing rings on the turbine throttle valves.

It seems that Dan's past experience at other plants led him to NOT take the generator off-line when there was a boiler trip. By taking the generator off-line, the plant would be charged for an Emergency Forced Outage. Bonanza Plant's EFOR (Emergency Forced Outage Rate) was already unacceptably high. By not removing the generator from the power grid while he purged and restarted the boiler, he could avoid

49

adding to the plant EFOR. This was a good idea right up until his ignorance did well over a million dollars worth of damage to the plant.

This was not an uncommon but entirely wrong practice at many plants. It is akin to Russian Roulette. You place one round in one of the six chambers and spin it several times. You have a 1 in 6 chance of dying. Dan later testified that he had done this numerous times at other plants because it was commonplace. Two things saved his job (this time):

1. He blamed his Control Room Operator. As his operator completed the boiler purge and put the fires back in the boiler, he opened the governor (control) valves on the turbine, increasing steam flow. He did not have a good explanation for why he did so. This increased the differential across the superheater pendants and the condensed water was carried out ('slugged') to the main steam line.

2. Because many plants practiced this operation depsite its danger, Dan was given a pass this time. Dan fully acted as if he knew the dangers of keeping the turbine running when the fires were out of the boiler. However, I knew he was completely full of crap. It was obviously the first time he had ever heard of this phenomenon when I brought it up immediately prior to the water induction incident. I wanted him fired but was overruled.

After a full investigation, we changed the control system to ensure that the cross-trip could not be defeated in the future. The plant was down for several weeks, assessing and repairing the damage. Even though I had tried to stop the incident from happening, Bob Culligan put tremendous pressure on me as it was additional, concrete evidence the plant had a severe training problem. I was the Training Manager; therefore, it fell onto my back.

After the Coleman water induction incident, I went into overdrive, putting a Utah State-certified apprenticeship in place at the plant. As one of the many mandated requirements of the apprenticeship, maintenance personnel were required to regularly come to my office and take written tests. Their job progression and raises were based largely upon my administration of the apprenticeship and their testing.

The apprenticeship was hastily designed and implemented because Bob wanted to control their raises and help flush some of the people out of the plant. His goal was to reduce plant staffing as quickly as possible, but was told by the Deseret upper management to allow *normal attrition* to make the reductions and not resort to active firings.

It didn't matter what they told him, Bob began putting tremendous pressure on the management and supervisory group at the plant. He insisted the Supervisors "police" people much harder and pushed for more output. As the pressure on everyone ratcheted upward, people began showing their hostility toward him by letting ME know that he was pushing too hard. Frankly, I loved the attention and continued to become even more self-inflated.

I even looked forward to my weekend "in the barrel." This is what they called the weekend coverage when you carried the pager. If there was a problem at the plant on weekends or holidays, there was always a dedicated management person carrying the pager. They were required to come to the plant when any incidents occurred or if the unit tripped. Most of the Managers hated it because you were required to stay in town (or at the plant) and "be available."

Not me... Carrying the pager made me feel incredibly important and fully indispensable.

Between Bob pulling me into his office on a continuous basis to "bounce something off of you" and me dealing with all the plant training issues and the apprenticeship, I felt like I was running the plant single-handedly. My ego continued to inflate much like a balloon. I wasn't intelligent or perceptive enough to realize that if a balloon over-inflates, *it pops*. My immaturity was absolutely stunning. I was now almost 31 years old. You would think I had matured beyond this by now.

My office was physically the very closest office to the plant and by far the noisiest. This meant that if the unit tripped, I heard it immediately. Bob Culligan, the real Plant Manager, had a digital megawatt meter in his quiet, stately office, but I had the intimate din and vibration of the plant equipment. Of course, Bob also had windows in his office, and his domain was professionally finished in classic brick and appropriately trendy sheetrock/hardwood trim that was sophistically decorated.

I had no windows other than the one in the gray metal door, and my office was made of cinderblock and painted beige. Yet, I still felt like the King and fully in charge. Looking back on it, I still do not comprehend how I could have been such a complete fool.

Proverbs 16:18 states, ***"Pride goeth before destruction, and a haughty spirit before a fall."*** I probably should have taken this one a little more to heart. It could have saved me, my family, and several other people a lot of heartache.

My morbidly obese ego changed how I viewed life in general. Realizing that I was an incredibly smart and powerful man, I could now set elevated standards for those around me. Since I was already doing this at work, the only other place I could allow my ego to manifest itself was at Church.

Even though we had lived through all the hell that took place at Garden City, First Assembly of God and saw, first-hand, the destruction and pain resulting from laypersons usurping their (selfish) wills upon the Pastor, I chose the identical path of destruction.

What's worse (much worse), I did it with self-perceived righteousness in my heart. Even today, it is extremely difficult and embarrassing to pen this... Far more than might be apparent. It is almost emotional to revisit this entire situation.

Stan and Karen Arias were great people. They would do anything for anyone and worked very hard to keep the doors open at the Vernal Assembly of God. Karen had to work at a local food store for them to make ends meet. However, they both ALWAYS had smiles on their faces, and their kids, Benjamin, Hillary, and Melissa, were always happy.

Because the Church was small and had been hit hard by the construction finishing at the power plant, the attendance was down from the previous few years. It enabled me to easily be elected to the elder board. The Church Board at most Assembly of God Churches was relatively powerful. It set the Pastor's salary, ensured the bills were paid, and ensured that the Church was currently on the right path now and in the foreseeable future.

Besides being on the Church Elder board, Vangie and I helped teach Sunday school to the younger age groups. This was supposed to be on a substitute basis but was quite regular due to the nature of the Church and people being absent for various reasons. We became friends with Stan and Karen and even took them to the lake a couple of times.

Stan was about 5'2" tall and immense in circumference. His hair had a distinctive "bowl" cut and was cropped at the top of his thick eyebrows. This, along with his thick, heavy mustache, made him resemble the Frito-Bandido.

He desperately wanted to water-ski, and Vangie did her very best to teach him. She was a consummate professional at teaching people to water-ski. I do not believe there was ever a person that she was not able to get up on skis... With one exception... *Stan Arias*. He was just too large and, on each successive try, would get as much as 50% out of the water, and his strength would wane, and down he would go.

On his best attempt, he was almost 70% out of the water. We were all cheering and certain he was making it up this time, but then the rope snapped with an unforgettable TWING!!! Brandi fell backward onto the floor as the boat lurched instantly forward at the loss of the dead weight when the rope snapped. It was very frustrating. Regardless, we had a nice time at the lake with the Arias family.

Despite of our friendship with Stan, the church was mediocre. Stan was a caring, loving Pastor but not necessarily a high-powered preacher. I was on the Church Elder board with four other men. One of them was Jonas Larson. Jonas and his wife, Norma, had been in the Church for several years. They had a daughter named Julie, who was about Vangie and I's age (30ish). Julie suffered severe and irreversible brain damage immediately after getting a vaccination as a baby. She could walk but had virtually no communication skills and was prone to frequent fits and outbursts. Julie appeared to have a mental age of about 18 months to 2 years old. Taking care of her was a constant difficulty for Jonas and Norma.

Jonas was a hardened and aggressive man in his mid to late 50's. He had worked in the oil patch all of his life. A few years before we arrived in Vernal, he designed a generic, reusable, concrete pump-jack platform that became extremely popular with the oil companies. He and their oldest son built a lucrative business around these platforms.

In an odd sort of way, Jonas and I were dealing with some of the same issues. The sudden onset of wealth through the pump-jack platforms provided Jonas with an abundance of pride and self-satisfaction. This, combined with his deep-seated anger over Julie's condition, made him a somewhat fearful figure in the Church. His son went to Church in Roosevelt, Utah, and it appeared their business partnership strained their relationship.

Because both of us perceived ourselves as giants in our field, we immediately hit it off. With our immense egos, unwarranted pride, and being on the Church Elder board, it was like mixing bleach and ammonia. The result is potentially lethal chloramine gas. Both of us being on the board at the same time almost became lethal to Pastor Stan Arias.

It started innocently enough. Jonas and I had a phone conversation about an upcoming board meeting. We were discussing what needed to be addressed at the Church. As our discussion matured, we concluded that we were uniquely able to correct any/all perceived issues in the Church and were morally obligated to do so.

More conversations ensued in the coming weeks. We determined by our immense, collective wisdom that if Stan

Arias were a more dynamic preacher, we could probably increase the size of the congregation ten-fold or more. We began putting intense pressure on Stan to, as we put it, "become more dynamic from the pulpit."

The more pressure we put on Stan, the harder he tried. However, he took our pressure with the grace and loving patience that only a saint could have displayed. Jonas then became openly hostile to Stan. He stopped hiding it in the board meetings and Church. I still did not see that what we were doing was morally *reprehensible*.

The final straw for us at the World Vision Assembly of God was a board meeting where Jonas openly requested a "vote of confidence" for retaining Pastor Arias. This was a simple majority vote that would either fire Stan or get the board (Jonas and I) off his back. It was tense, awkward, decidedly wrong, and Stan had three votes of confidence and two votes of no confidence. Thank God Jonas and I were outvoted.

Immediately after the vote, Jonas resigned from the board and decided to attend the Church his son was attending in Roosevelt, Utah. I stayed on the board for a few days and then resigned because I could not look Stan Arias in the eyes. Deep in my spirit, I finally knew what I was doing was just plain wrong.

After leaving the Church board at World Vision Assembly, Vangie and I decided to drive to Grand Junction, Colorado, and go to Church every chance we could. We discovered Redlands Faith Assembly. It was being pastored by a man and his wife named Samuel and Nancy Brassfield.

They were both very dynamic, and the Church was amazing. The worship was above and beyond any place we had ever attended. It was reminiscent of the feelings we had years earlier when we worshiped in Wheatland, Wyoming, with Mel Bindas leading the worship at Alliance Faith Chapel.

We felt bad that Brandi, Brittanie, and Josh could not go to Church every week like they did when we attended World Vision Assembly of God, but we felt regenerated and renewed after we visited the Redlands Faith Assembly.

Unfortunately, as I had observed in the past when the spiritual goes awry, *EVERYTHING* goes awry. I did not realize that with my horrible performance at Church, I had opened the door to problems I never dreamed of prior to this.

During this same period, I received a very simple powerplant simulator demo from Leighton and Kidd out of Canada. It was neatly packaged with a 5 1/4" floppy disk and would run quite well without being loaded onto a hard drive. Hard drives were becoming more prevalent but were still in short supply due to the price. It was called the I.S.S (Interactive Simulation System) and effectively taught the fundamentals of power plant physics.

It cost around $250.00 to purchase. I was going to buy it and put it in the plant library, but I never got around to it due to the extreme and exhausting pace I was keeping at the plant. What I did not realize in 1987 is that not too many years later, this product would play a profound and life-changing role in our lives.

CHAPTER 6

THE CULLIGAN CONUNDRUM

Bob Culligan hated Mormons. There was not much more to say than this. Even though he was told to reduce staffing by attrition, he was prone to firing someone for the smallest infraction if they met a primary vetting parameter… Being Mormon. What's more, he was out to get Stan Gorman. Stan was the Operations Superintendent and would have unquestionably, been promoted to Plant Manager, except he made a major error early in the start-up of the plant.

Remember Juan Archuleta, the Training Manager at Intermountain Power Plant ,who spoke 'Spanglish'? (He was the one that I could barely understand because of his Spanish accent). Anyway, Stan Gorman married his sister. Her name was Nora Archuleta, and they had children together. Early in the start-up of the Bonanza Plant, Stan 'accidentally' had an affair with one of the secretaries at the plant named Beth Hamilton and promptly dumped Nora for her. While not good in the Mormon Church, it was excusable. However, it cost him the Plant Manager's job. Up until then, he was unquestionably the fair-haired boy at the plant.

I liked Stan. Beth obviously liked Stan. Frankly, everyone liked Stan except Bob Culligan. Stan was a 'dyed-in-the-wool' Mormon, vexing Bob to no end. However, Stan was truly a gentle giant. He was about 6'4" tall and smart as a whip. To me, his biggest personal flaw was practicing the Utah Power and Light way of doing things and dumping his wife and kids for Beth.

Bob was zeroing in Stan. He wanted to fire him so badly he could taste it. His primary complaint about Stan was he was indecisive and slow to action. What was the real reason he wanted to fire him? Stan was Mormon and forbidden fruit. Deseret's upper management wanted him groomed to replace Bob. This irked Bob to no end. Since I felt certain Bob would make me the new Operations Superintendent if he fired Stan, I became a willing and eager pawn in his crusade.

In reality, I doubt I would have ever been promoted to Stan's job, but I was so seriously compromised by the whole enormous ego issue I couldn't see reality if it fell on my head like a cinderblock from heaven.

It became increasingly clear that Bob had serious flaws. I didn't want to see them. I even denied them. I explained them away in my mind. I defended him to the plant personnel like a dedicated fireman combats a raging fire. However, it was becoming increasingly clear... *Bob had major issues.*

He seemed to have a death wish for Mormons, and he absolutely despised the Deseret upper management. On several occasions, he commented to me how ludicrous, ignorant, and repulsive his boss, Warren Franklin, and the head of Deseret, Merrill Miller, were.

Bob was incredibly smart and knew all the right things to say, but his sinister side was unrelenting and now seemed to be dominating his entire plan for "cleaning up the plant".

Bob became openly, obnoxiously hostile to Stan in the morning meetings. He constantly set up Stan to fail by quietly dispatching me to find minor details about specific, usually minor, issues in the plant prior to the meetings. I would immediately run out into the plant and delve into the situation as quickly as possible, providing explicit details to Bob immediately before a meeting.

Bob would then cold-cock and assault Stan for not having intimate knowledge of the issue. Most of the time, Stan wouldn't even know something was happening until Bob absolutely hammered him with it in the meeting. It was entirely a set-up each time. Stan was always stoic and accepting of Bob's verbal abuse. Stan was like the constantly battered wife who would tell authorities that she "deserved it."

Oddly, I know Stan was communicating directly with Warren Franklin and the Deseret upper management in a completely stealth manner. It was in their Mormon DNA to do so. Bob had to of known it. He didn't seem to care in the least. He was verbally pummeling Stan at every opportunity.

In an odd, amusing sort of way, Bob and Stan were alike in most of their opinions and views. Bob did not like women in the plant, and neither did Stan. Neither of them cared for lazy people in the plant, but Stan would tolerate more than Bob. Both felt personnel training levels were critically important. Both focused on the same pertinent metrics to gauge the plant's performance. The difference being Stan was Mormon and very smart. This seemed to incense Bob.

Stan had one of the most droll, ludicrous sense of humors of anyone I ever knew. On January 28th, 1986, the space shuttle Challenger exploded moments after lift-off, tragically killing all seven astronauts. Later that day, I walked into Stan's office to ask him a question. Before I could speak, he looked at me very seriously and quietly said, "They just released the final words of the Challenger commander." He seemed truly disturbed.

"What were they?" I asked empathetically. It was obviously troubling him.

His round face then took on an air of mirth as he said, *"No! I said Bud Light."*

In the mid-1980s, Anheuser-Busch, the manufacturer of Budweiser beer, had a long run of commercials where someone would ask for a "light" (referring to beer), and he/she would then be handed something totally ridiculous (usually on fire) and then the character in the commercial would say, *"No! I said Bud Light!"* Stan always had an absurd joke or pun to tender in every situation. This was typical.

It was shortly after this I ran afoul of both Bob and Stan. There was an Auxiliary Operator in the plant named Lisa Edwards. She was a tiny slip of a girl with red hair, horn-rim glasses, and a very prominent proboscis. She was quite intelligent and worked her tail off to move up in the plant. She was also young, unmarried, and had a daughter about 10 years old.

We had a complex promotional system at the plant that we called the matrix. It numerically evaluated several factors in the quest to find the best person for a position. We weighted and provided numerical scoring values for numerous parameters to determine the best person for a job. These scoring parameters included time in their current position, completion of the required qualification material, attendance record, disciplinary record, interview strength, and testing scores.

Testing was provided by an oral board that consisted of two management personnel. It was usually Stan and I, but we could substitute others of our choosing. On test day, the promotional candidate would reach into a pliable felt bag and randomly draw ten pieces of brass, placing them on the table.

Each piece of brass was stamped with a number that coincided with an exam question for the open position.

I intentionally published and provided the plant personnel with 100 possible questions (without the answers) for the control room operator exam. Because of this, the job candidate couldn't say the question was a surprise because they had access to all of them. They just didn't know which 10 of the 100 they would pick.

The oral board would then ask the question and force the applicant to explain everything they knew about the question in vivid, accurate detail. When complete, both the oral board testers would provide a score between 0% and 100%, reflecting their opinion of how well they answered the question. The random drawing of brass tags was completely objective but was nullified by the scoring that always proved to be totally subjective.

Neither Stan nor Bob wanted Lisa to be promoted to Control Room Operator. They both felt she would be a hazard on the job due to her "immaturity and fragile emotional state." I was told by Bob to score hard and ensure that one of the men she was competing with was rewarded with the job. As Training Manager, I was the overseer and administrator of the entire promotional process.

On the fateful day of her testing, Lisa arrived for her oral board exam loaded for bear. She was very smart and had studied an extraordinary amount for the control room operator position. We spent over *four hours* with her on an exam that normally took about an hour. We could not stump her. When all three of us were completely exhausted, Stan and I excused her from the conference room and compared our scores. Stan scored her at 35%. I scored her at 98%.

"Stan, how could you give her 35%?" I asked indignantly.

Stan's normally jolly demeanor turned deadly serious.

"I don't want her in my control room. She can't handle pressure, and she will get no respect from her crew."

I opened my notebook and looked at her overall scoring parameters in the matrix. She was virtually perfect. We had never had someone do better in all the scorable areas. I looked back at Stan.

"We can't deny her this position. The promotional matrix that *YOU* approved and helped develop is designed to prevent what you are trying to do."

Stan was unyielding. He looked straight into my eyes and stated ominously, "Doesn't matter... She WILL be the exception. She is not getting into my control room while I am the Operations Superintendent." His jaw was set, and he appeared resolute. He then gave me an irritated look and wryly said, "I think we should let Culligan be the tie-breaker on this one."

Stan was smart, and he knew Bob did not want her in the control room any more than he did. Oddly, he did not have to appeal to Bob because, technically, he had the final say. The entire reason for his appeal to Bob was to punish *me*. He knew all along how Bob was using me to get to him.

Lisa's test took so long that the office crew was preparing to leave for the day. However, Bob was still in his office when Stan gently knocked on his open door.

"Can we have a quick word with you?" Stan asked quietly in his typical low-key fashion.

"Come in. What's on your mind?" Bob leaned waaaay back in his chair and clasped his hands behind his head. It was the end of the day, and he looked fatigued. Bob knew Lisa's test took far too long because he walked conspicuously by the conference room several times while impatiently eyeing our progress. However, he now had a look of satisfaction on his face. I could tell he was expecting the ultimate announcement that Lisa failed and would not get the control room operator job.

Stan looked at Bob with an air of concern on his face.

"I gave Lisa a 35% on the oral testing, and Mark gave her 98%." He paused and then looked skeptically at me. "Mark is saying Lisa passed the matrix, beating the competition, and now we have to give her the job." He paused again, looked back at Bob, and said, "You are going to have to be the tie-breaker here."

As smart as Stan was, he *grossly* underestimated the malevolent and scheming Bob Culligan. It is surprising that he did so because he already knew how Bob was undercutting him at every opportunity. I am certain he felt Bob would wholly agree with him about not putting Lisa in the control room, thus shaming and forcing me to do something I disagreed with. We were both caught wholly off-guard by Bob's intense response.

He immediately sat straight up in his chair and plopped his hands flat on his desk with a loud slap.

"Stan, **YOU** have the final say because she works in **YOUR** department." His voice dropped an octave, and his eyes squinted. "As usual, you cannot make a decision to save your damn life." He looked at me angrily. "Mark, what do you

64

think will happen if we deny her this job?" I was surprised he turned to me so quickly.

"Well," I stammered...

Before I could finish answering, he stood up and exclaimed, "I'll tell you what is going to happen... That little bitch will get a lawyer, and it will be rammed up our ass." He was yelling now. "As far as I am concerned, you BOTH screwed up royally. You have no choice but to give her the damn job!"

Bob stared at the two of us without flinching. He was good at this, the best I ever knew. He could drop the hammer on someone and, regardless of how awkward and uncomfortable the situation was, still stare you straight in the face, his eyes glaring with righteous indignation.

Stan pulled a typical 'Stan-move' and turned to me quietly, saying, "I guess you won this one. We need to give her the job." He was void of emotion and had an expression of total disconnect on his face. We both turned and left the office. There was no other word said about Bob's eruption.

The next day, we announced that Lisa was awarded the Control Operator position. She was thrilled, and Stan was hacked at me. Bob didn't mention it further and acted like I did well. I think he was happy to have another reason to yell and belittle Stan. The entire situation was simply as screwed-up as it could possibly be.

The next major incident that fully convinced me I had hitched my wagon to a falling star was a junket Bob arranged for Jim Hastings, a plant maintenance supervisor, and me. We were to visit a couple of Bob's old charges in North Dakota.

One was the Stanton Energy Center, and the other was the mighty Coal Creek Plant.

He took Jim Hastings because he was a great guy, and Bob didn't perceive him as Mormon. It turns out he was, but he was very low-key. I *really* liked Jim. He was honest, straightforward, sharp, and a good maintenance supervisor. Obviously, Stan was not invited on this trip due to Bob's loathing of him.

We flew into Bismarck, North Dakota, and rented a car. We were staying at a Best Western Inn in Beulah, North Dakota. It was a tiny, windswept burg that consisted of a few stores and a hotel/restaurant that stayed in business only because of all the power plants in the area.

Central North Dakota is rich in lignite reserves. Lignite is very low-grade, 'brown' coal. Technically, it was not considered coal due to its low heating value and color. However, everyone outside of the industry called it coal. The lignite was easy to reach, so all the mines were surface strip mines. After being burned, the ash from these plants would be returned to the strip mines to support reclamation efforts.

Because the lignite heating value is so low, the plant boilers in the area were enormous due to handling the tremendous burn rate necessary to achieve their designed electrical loads. Indeed, Coal Creek's two boilers were physically the largest boilers in the world but only produced 550 MW each. In comparison, there are single-unit, 1200 MW plants in the eastern part of the country with smaller boilers than Coal Creek because they burn 12,000+ BTU/Lb coal versus Coal Creek's barely 5,000 BTU/Lb lignite.

The staggering number of lignite plants clustered in North Dakota made it power plant heaven. All the plants were large due to the lignite fuel; most were multi-unit plants. In 1986, the following large plants were located in a 150-mile radius of Bismarck:

- Heskett Station

- Coal Creek Station

- Leland Olds Station

- Stanton Energy Center

- Square Butte (Minnkota) Station

- Coyote Station

- Antelope Valley Station

The combined output of these plants was far more than the entire state of North Dakota ever used on a yearly basis. Most of the power output from these plants went to surrounding states.

I was thrilled to accompany Bob to his old plants and see these enormous, fire-breathing monsters. It was no surprise that Bob was drinking heavily *prior* to boarding the Delta Airlines 737 jet in Salt Lake City. He paid for a couple of more drinks on the flight to Bismarck. The more he imbibed, the louder and more obnoxious he became.

We rented a car at Bismarck Airport and drove the hour-long drive to Beulah. The entire area is desolate, cold, and flat. However, my heart would race as we saw the stacks of the various plants off in the distance. Bob was a consummate storyteller and kept us entertained the entire way to Beulah.

The more inebriated he was, the better the stories became because truth was not a factor in any of them.

When we arrived at the hotel, he told us to meet him for dinner in the restaurant after we had unpacked and settled in the room. When Jim and I arrived at the restaurant, Bob was at a table with an empty cocktail glass. I am certain this was already his second drink since it took Jim and me about 15 minutes to get back to the restaurant.

He launched back into his tall tales with inebriated exuberance. He was fun to listen to and quite humorous, although as his blood alcohol level increased, so did the profanity and darkness of the stories.

When the youthful and comely waitress came to take our order, he began giving her a hard time and then pinched her on the rear. You could tell she was irritated but still handled it professionally. I am certain this was far from her first encounter with a drunk. I am also certain being a drunk was a prerequisite for living in Beulah, North Dakota, in the winter.

As soon as she left our table, I made the mistake of chastising Bob for his obnoxious behavior.

"Don, you better be careful, someday, a waitress is going to do a tap dance on your head."

Bob looked at me and grinned sloppily, crassly replying, "That sweet young thing, she would never do anything like that!" He then looked over to a table near ours that had what looked like a 60+-year-old leather-faced farmer and his large, heavy-set, sun-aged wife at his side. "Now that old battle axe sitting there, she could do you some serious damage!"

68

He said it far loud enough for them to hear. Jim and I were completely mortified. I locked eyes with Jim and without saying a word, we both knew that we wanted out of there as soon as possible.

Unfortunately, he was just getting started. The more he drank, the more obnoxious he became. He ordered a sirloin steak dinner. As he ate and embellished stories we had already heard, his plate was slowly moving off the table. During a stab of his fork into the steak to hold it while he cut it, the plate flipped up and deposited its contents directly onto his lap.

Bob immediately jumped up and hollered, "Would it be possible to get a knife sharp enough to cut this crappy steak!" The waitress hurried over with a towel as Bob scraped the remaining mashed potatoes off his lap and onto the plate. "Hey there, little girl, can you clean my lap with that towel." He had a lecherous grin on his face. Now, it was her turn to be obnoxious.

"Listen, old man, you can quietly finish eating, or you can leave. Another word from you, and I will have the Manager throw you out along with the mess you just made."

He tilted his head back and looked at her through his bifocals and slurred, "That wasn't a nice thing to say to a paying guest at this establishment!" She didn't flinch.

"I've had enough of you, you're out of here." She turned and quickly exited to the back of the restaurant. Moments later, the manager followed her back out to the table. He was heavy set, balding, and looked to be in his forties. While not particularly mean-looking, I wouldn't want to tangle with him.

"Sir, I must ask you to leave. I understand you are staying here. You need to go to your room… *Now!*" He then looked at Jim and me.

Jim immediately answered, "We are sorry about this. We will get him to his room."

"This is bullshit!" Bob retorted. We were worried he was going to make an even larger scene because he was now an angry drunk. However, Jim handled things extremely well. He quickly and effectively put his arm around him and coerced, more like drug, him out the front door of the restaurant.

I stayed long enough to apologize profusely and pay the bill. The waitress got an extra big tip from us that night. Jim and I didn't speak much about the events of the evening, but we exchanged enough concerned glances while it was happening to know we were both appalled at Bob's actions. Unfortunately, the trip was far from over.

The visit to Bob's previous plants was great. He was relatively quiet and never mentioned what happened at the restaurant. It was obvious he was here just to visit with old friends. Jim and I made good use of the time talking to the people in our positions and seeing their programs.

The remaining day in North Dakota went quickly, and Jim and I were convinced that the visit would be beneficial to us. Bob seemed happy just to visit with all his old friends. The second night, he again drank very hard. While obnoxious, he did not repeat the train wreck of the first night. Unfortunately, the trip home was a different story.

We boarded the 737 back to Salt Lake City late in the afternoon. Bob was already drinking heavily before boarding the plane. After take-off, he bought at least two more drinks that I know of. He was feeling no pain when we made our final approach to Salt Lake Airport.

I had flown enough with Engineering Physics to know something wasn't right. We did a close fly-by and then did the approach but did not actually touch down. I knew then something wasn't right at all. The pilot was very professional and managed our anxiety well.

"Folks, this is Captain Riggs." His voice was upbeat and strong. "We do not show the nose wheel being down and locked. We did a fly-by, and the ground personnel have confirmed the nose wheel is down. However, the 737 does not have fuel dumping capabilities, so we must burn off some fuel before touching down." He paused. "Please do not be alarmed. We are certain there is no issue, and we are required to follow certain guidelines set forth by the FAA."

Bob immediately reached up and rang the flight attendant call button. It took a few minutes for the flight attendant to get to our seats. "May I help you, sir?" She was in her 30's and was also very professional.

"I would like a bourbon, please." He was intense.

"I'm sorry, sir, there is no cabin service at this time."

"That's bullshit."

She was unruffled. "Sir, please sit back and relax; everything is going to be fine." She immediately turned and went back to the front of the plane.

I was waiting for Bob to give an angry outburst, but he sat quietly, looking totally tense.

We flew a wide circular pattern for about 45 minutes. On our final approach to the airport, we could see the emergency equipment's flashing lights lining the runway, increasing our anxiety.

"Folks, Captain Riggs here." His voice was again upbeat, professional, and confident, which is exactly what you need in this situation. "We are certain the nose gear is locked, and the landing will be without incident. However, I am going to land the plane and hold the nose high. At the last minute, I will drop the nose of the aircraft, and if the nose gear is not locked, you will hear loud scraping and some vibration in the cabin. Even if it is not locked, it should not be a major issue for the passengers. Simply follow the directions of the flight attendants and exit the plane. There should be no major issue."

Captain Riggs had barely finished when Culligan shouted aloud, "What the hell do you mean, NO ISSUE! *It sounds like a damn plane crash to me!*" A woman in the row in front of us let out a muffled yelp, almost like a dog whose tail was inadvertently stepped on. I was again mortified at Bob as the Flight Attendants converged on our row.

Bob was in the aisle seat, and the young lady who attended him earlier knelt next to him and, with venom in her voice, emphatically stated, "Sir, that was uncalled for, and you need to keep your mouth closed and let us do our jobs!" I realized then that Bob had lost most of the color in his face. He just stared at her and didn't say anything further.

Other than the flashing lights from the emergency vehicles lining the runway, the landing was smooth and without incident. The nose wheel was obviously locked.

After the trip to North Dakota, Bob started dropping more responsibilities on me. Besides the documentation projects, and the training and apprenticeship administration, he was assigning me to the Root Cause Analysis (RCA) team every time the unit tripped or had an incident.

While I was concerned about his agenda and motives, I felt more secure in the knowledge that I was absolutely indispensable at the Bonanza Plant. Unfortunately, it was a mirage generated by pride and a completely unchecked ego. I couldn't see it at the time, but I am certain I was treated with the kid gloves by plant personnel who knew I was a direct line to Bob Culligan.

I was little more than a suggestion box with a pulse. I was nailed to a wall where employees would dump their suggestions with the hope that they might be read and acted upon by someone with authority to do so. *That was certainly not me.*

December 1986 came quickly, and with it was Bob Culligan's final assault on Deseret G&T. The plant had its own Christmas celebration and parties, but the corporate Christmas Party for upper management was held at a very nice restaurant in the Salt Lake City area. Bob was invited to the corporate Christmas party and asked me if I would accompany him and his wife, Flo, to the dinner.

The reality of the situation was simple: Bob wanted to drink, and Flo didn't like driving, so I chauffeured them on the three-hour drive to Sandy and back. No problem. To the plant personnel (and me), it appeared that I was still the fair-haired boy at the plant, as well as Bob's confidant.

We arrived at the opulent event that included Merrill Miller, the General Manager (CEO) of the cooperative, and the entire upper management from the Deseret headquarters. Everyone was dressed to the gills, and it was a lavish, professional setting for a Christmas Party. The only missing element was an open bar. There was not a soul at the event that would dare have an adult beverage because there was little separation between the Mormon Church and the Deseret management group.

I stopped drinking when we were in Farmington and was certainly not offended by the lack of alcohol at the event. Bob was incensed. He seemed to unhinge when he realized it was a 'dry' party. So much so that he went out of his way to secure cocktails for himself and Flo at his own cost. The Deseret Managers were gracious and did not make any issue of him and Flo drinking. Unfortunately, they did not know what I knew about Bob's drinking issues.

I was hoping Bob would hold his alcohol intake to one or two cocktails. I was chagrined that he had those down before the appetizer round was finished. As the dinner entre was being served, his complexion was already flushed, and he continued drinking. I had a sick feeling deep in the pit of my stomach. I knew this was not going to end well. Unfortunately, it was far worse than I could have ever imagined.

The party was low-key and comfortable. The food was excellent, but Bob was completely inebriated. About halfway through the entire course of dinner, he raised his voice and got everyone's attention.

Before continuing, I must warn that the discourses from Bob at this party were crude, obnoxious, and not suitable for younger or sensitive readers. *If you are easily offended, please skip the rest of this chapter because it is/was not pretty. Seriously, it was bad. I am offering this almost verbatim. Again, if you are sensitive, don't read further. Just suffice it to say that Bob made a fool of himself and seriously angered everyone in the room, including me.*

Out of the clear blue, with no provocation, Bob raised his voice loud enough that everyone stopped talking and gave him the floor.

He began loudly, "You know, I remember a Christmas several years ago when Flo and I were a bit younger." He turned and looked at Flo, raising his cocktail glass and nodding his head at her.

"Flo lovingly looked at me and said, Bob, kiss me where it is warm and moist." He paused and grinned widely. "I said, okay honey, and I took her to Beaumont."

I instantly went numb as I saw the horror on the faces of everyone in the restaurant. You could hear a pin drop. Time ground to a halt, and everyone just stared at Bob. Seeing he had their attention, he belligerently continued.

"Did you all hear about the gal who went on a fishing expedition with a bunch of male sailors?" He paused and donned a sinister grin. "She came back with a Red Snapper. When they asked her why she did it, she said just for the halibut."

He then cracked up laughing. Flo immediately jerked his arm, pulling him over to her. She whispered in his ear for a few moments. His countenance quickly turned violent as he pulled back and said, "I didn't say a damn thing wrong. It was just good humor. If they don't like it, it's their problem."

Flo went crimson red and looked completely disgusted as she pushed her chair back and quickly exited the dinner area with her face down. It appeared she was headed in the direction of the restrooms. I didn't know what to do. Merrill Miller and most of the Managers had a look of death on their faces. The mood in the restaurant turned dark and extremely pained. Bob was the only one who acted like nothing ever happened as he picked at his food with a malignant grin on his face.

I immediately got up and went back to the restroom area to check on Flo. She was nowhere to be found. I wasn't sure what to do. I waited for a few minutes to see if she would come out of the restroom when Bob wandered back, looked angrily at me, and then banged his fist on the restroom door.

"Flo, dammit, are you in there?" he hollered loudly. A moment later the restroom door cracked open, and I could see Flo crying.

She addressed ME and not Bob. "Could you please take me back to the hotel? I am not feeling well."

Bob looked at me and angrily said, "Take us both back to the hotel. I am done here."

I didn't even bother going back into the party hall. The damage was done, and the best thing I could do was get them out of there. I knew then that the party was over. I am not talking about the Christmas party. I knew Bob was finished at Deseret.

The three-hour drive back to Vernal the next morning was horribly awkward and emotionally draining. Bob would normally have verbal diarrhea, but now wasn't speaking to Flo or me. Flo wouldn't speak or even look at either of us.

As it turned out, Bob already had another job lined up. He had been offered the Plant Manager position at the Hugo Power Plant owned by Western Farmers Electric Cooperative in Hugo, Oklahoma. The Hugo Plant was the same size as Bonanza but a couple of years older. He would be the plant's second Plant Manager as the first one retired. Apparently, his crass and vulgar actions at the Christmas party were his going-away gift to the Deseret management he hated so badly. *Gee, thanks, Bob. We all needed this.*

CHAPTER 7

A DARK AND COLD PLACE

The corporate Christmas party convinced me I was in big trouble at the plant. I didn't have a clue just how much so until Bob gave his resignation a week later. The plant was immediately abuzz about his replacement. After the word spread that he was resigning, an odd and troubling trend occurred. Numerous people began dropping by my office and cynically wanting to know when I was following Bob to Oklahoma.

Though not very bright, I quickly realized I was a complete pariah at the plant. Whether people liked or disliked Bob, it didn't change the way most of them looked at me. It became obvious I was viewed as an extraneous snitch or evil minion for the all-powerful Culligan... The same Culligan who just burned his bridges at Deseret was now leaving me high and dry and out in the cold.

What made this even worse? Up until the very end, I was a willing volunteer (stooge) for his evil agenda. It is so difficult to reflect upon this. I have repented more times than anyone can imagine for my role in this entire disgusting, appalling situation.

Deseret immediately placed an advertisement for a Plant Manager in Power Engineering and Power Magazine. Most of the Mormons thought they would simply award the job to Stan.

Eventually, Stan would get the Plant Manager's position, but they had to cycle through one more Plant Manager. After several interviews with potential candidates, they interviewed Bob York. Yes, the same Bob York I worked for/with at Engineering Physics—the Englishman whose nose, ears, and face had been customized by years of Rugby.

Warren Franklin and the corporate officers in Sandy apparently were quite impressed with Bob. They extended him an offer that he couldn't refuse. I would like to think I had something to do with this because I made sure they understood that he almost walked on water. I thought if there was a chance to salvage my career at Bonanza Plant, he was it. Fortunately, they did not hold it against him that we knew each other.

I could barely contain my excitement about Bob coming on board. Vangie and I scoped out the area and gave him numerous pointers on the best places to live. He seemed appreciative of our input.

Immediately after arriving, he treated me exactly as he had at Engineering Physics… A professional colleague who shared similar goals. Unfortunately, this radically and rapidly changed after he started work at the plant.

Bob's first quest was to bring every single one of the 125 or so employees into his office, one by one, and get to know them and find out what they did at the plant. He had the executive secretary, Carlene, take their pictures and arrange them on a board so he could remember each one. Everyone thought it was a great start for a new Plant Manager. It took most of his first two weeks to talk to every plant employee.

I was the last one to come to his office for 'the talk' because he, of course, already knew me. It was in this meeting that I had my heart summarily ripped out, diced, and returned to me with venom. The very moment I walked into his office and saw his face, I knew something was wrong… Way, way wrong. I shouldn't have been surprised by it. I knew I was a pariah, but I was so screwed up that I honestly thought Bob was going to restore me to my previously exalted position.

"Have a seat, Mark." His speech was measured, his tone succinct. "As you know, I have met virtually every person on this plant site and discussed my intended direction for the plant along with their concerns for the future."

I smiled carefully, looked him directly in the eyes and said, "I think this was an excellent idea and a great way to commence your responsibilities as the manager of this plant."

His demeanor turned dark. "I am so glad you approve." His sarcasm was not lost on me.

"You were the inadvertent subject of many conversations this week and not just with employees here at the plant." His voice was steady, purposeful, and grim. "Between here and Sandy, the consensus is that you have been out of control and running unchecked in this plant." He paused to watch my reaction. I sat frozen, numb, trying to aspirate normally and show as little emotion as possible.

"Bob Culligan didn't do me any favors." I tried to keep my voice steely, cold, and unflinching.

"I'm sure he didn't." He shook his head slowly and continued, "However, you shouldn't have been so willing to participate in his games."

I could feel rage stirring within my gut. My face went flush and hot as I carefully defended myself. "I simply did what I was told. I was a new employee and earnestly asked by my new boss to help him correct problems in this plant." A sickening knot was forming in my stomach as I continued.

"Did anyone happen to mention that I have rewritten most of the unusable plant documentation to be usable in an incredibly short period of time?" Before he could answer, I raised my voice, visibly trying to keep it from shaking as rage welled up within me.

"Did anyone bother to mention that I also implemented a full Utah State Certified apprenticeship for the maintenance crafts in the same incredibly short period of time? Do you have a clue how much work that took? Do you even have the slightest idea of how many hours I have invested in putting together a massive training plan for the operations department and all of the crafts in this plant?" I felt myself wanting to reach across the desk and put my fist into his already battered face.

He stiffened up in his chair, looked at me angrily and said, "You calm down NOW!" His emphasis on the "NOW!"

shocked me enough that I pulled back. I just glared at him and waited for his next move.

"Mark, I know you better than you think. I know you are a hard worker, enthusiastic, and smart." He leaned forward in his chair, carefully spread his hands and pleaded. "That isn't the point, though. The point is, you are perceived as a worm that would do anything for Culligan, no matter what you were asked."

I felt defiled and violated. I sat back in my chair, shocked, deflated, and sick to my stomach. I realized at that moment I was done. I stared at Bob for a few moments and, with complete surrender, said, "Do you want my resignation?"

To my surprise, he answered with a glimmer of hope on his face. "No, not at all. I need your skills. You can be a tremendous asset to this plant if we can get past all this Culligan garbage." He paused and shook his head again. "I need you to reset and go back to your office and become the Training Supervisor and not the assistant or pseudo, plant manager. I need you to do what you were hired to do." He drew a quick breath. "I know you are capable of doing it so this whole thing can eventually blow over."

I felt exhausted on an existential level. I stared at him and, with total resignation said, "I will do the best I can for you just as I did for Culligan."

"Great!" He lightly popped his right fist down on the desk. "Do you fully understand what I am asking you to do?" He looked at me, expecting an answer that wasn't going to happen. I just stared at him with an empty soul.

His eyes then flashed anger as he said, "I need you to be the damn Training Supervisor of this plant and provide training everywhere it is needed, and absolutely *nothing* else. This is what you are being paid to do."

I thought about it for a moment and then blandly said, "Do you still want me to participate in the morning meetings and do weekend duty when my turn rolls around?"

"Are either of those things training-related?"

"Nope, not all," I answered tersely.

"There's your answer and your charge. You will do training and nothing but training until everything blows over, and you can prove you are something more than just a henchman for Culligan."

"You got it," I said quietly. "I will do my best to change the plant's perception of me." I was numb and entirely uncaring at this point. I was unfamiliar with getting my wings clipped. *It felt like total crap.*

"Anything else?" I asked with complete surrender.

"I know you are pissed. Why don't you take tomorrow off and get your head screwed on straight? Come back Monday and help me clean up this plant the proper way and not the Culligan way."

He stood and held out his right hand. I slowly stood and shook it as I quietly said, "Thanks, Bob. I won't let you down. I will get it together." I was being completely disingenuous. I just wanted to walk out of this plant and never step foot back into it again. I felt completely broken and defeated.

In reality, I should have been thankful I still had a job. At that moment, I still did not fully see what I had done to myself, but another heavy dose of reality was right around the corner.

82

I took the next day off as Bob suggested. It was a Friday. I was moping around the house and being a general sad sack. Vangie knew about most of Culligan's recent actions and a little bit about my meeting with Bob York. Unfortunately, her view of what was happening was entirely through my eyes and was void of reality. I certainly did not want the woman I adored and whom I dedicated my life to, to see I was seriously compromised by my own pride and ego.

As always, she knew me better than I knew myself. She saw the way I was acting at Church with Jonas Larson. She knew how I had turned on Stan Arias. She saw the ego and pride I was walking in. She would not come out and say it, but I think she was aware the picture I was painting was not the picture of reality but a view tainted by my rose-colored glasses. She had been down this road with me in one form or another too many times already.

"Marko," she playfully called out to me about mid-morning. "Why don't you run to the market and get some hamburger and buns, and let's do burgers on the grill this afternoon." She was doing her best to try and lift my spirits from the beating I took on Thursday.

"Okay, sounds fine to me." I was still feeling deeply sorry for myself. I left the house and decided to go to the smaller IGA market near our house and not all the way to Smith's on the other side of town. We had been avoiding this market because Karen Arias was a clerk there and my guilty conscience made it difficult for me to see her.

I got a package of hamburger buns and some hamburger meat and proceeded to the front of the store to check out. As luck (or God) would have it, there was only one check-out clerk at that moment.

It was Karen Arias.

I didn't feel like facing her, but I had no choice. I even considered putting the food back and going to Smith's to avoid passing through Karen's checkout line. However, she always pleasant and had a sunny disposition. Because of this, I told myself it was going to be okay.

I put my food on her small, black conveyor belt as she checked out the lady in front of me. When she finished with her, she looked up and our eyes locked. A look of horror that quickly morphed into despair permeated her countenance. As her eyes filled with pain, tears immediately began streaming down her cheeks. She sharply punched the price of the buns and hamburger into her cash register and would not look at me again, turning away as she sobbed, "$2.29."

At that very moment, a single, brief moment in time that will always be painfully etched into my memory, I realized what I had become. The back of my throat clenched, and I could feel tears forming in my eyes.

I quickly put $3.00 on the platform by her register and haltingly said, "Karen... I am soooo sorry..."

I grabbed the hamburger and buns and bolted from the store, not waiting for my 71 cents. I barely made it to the car before I was overwhelmed with emotion. In that one moment, it hit me. In one fleeting moment, I realized what a cowardly weasel I had become. I saw the sheer pain and intense hurt she had suffered by my hand. I immediately thought back to the pain and suffering Gordon and Lois Nelson experienced during their ordeal in Garden City and how I felt towards the people who hurt them. My cheeks were stinging from the acidic, hot tears streaming down my face.

84

I realized that I did to Stan and Karen Arias precisely what those people I abhorred in Garden City did to Gordon and Lois Nelson. Just as Judas betrayed Christ with a kiss, I befriended Stan and Karen and then stabbed them right square in the heart.

Why? I reasoned. Why did I do this? Pastor Stan was a great guy. He loved the Lord and worked hard to simply love people and further the Gospel of Christ. He was a Godly, Bible-preaching Pastor that loved his congregation and was dedicated to his wife and kids. Where was my mind? How could I have done what I did?

My thoughts were spinning out of control. I then realized that, in a weird, twisted sort of way, I did the same thing to Stan Gorman. I allowed Culligan to use me as a hammer against Stan. Sadly, it was not because Stan was terrible at his job but because Stan was Mormon and Culligan hated Mormons.

The floodgates of embarrassment opened as I became self-aware of everything I had become. At that moment, I felt that I could never look into the eyes of any of the plant personnel or our former Church family again. *I am not sure I could even look at myself in a mirror.*

I knew then I had to do something. It was now fully apparent. *We had to leave Vernal.* It was a simple equation only solved by leaving Vernal and never looking back.

I drove around Vernal, allowing my eyes to dry, and regained my composure before going home to do the burgers. The remainder of the weekend was miserable. Vangie was completely fed up with me by the time Sunday evening rolled around.

Returning to the plant Monday morning, I was in my office and trying as hard as possible to stay invisible. I was making phone calls looking for another plant that would hire me. I noticed in Power Magazine that there were several cogeneration facilities being commissioned all over the country, and Burns and McDonnell was doing the engineering at many of them. Most of these facilities were cogeneration plants.

Cogeneration is a term for a power plant that is tied directly to a plant process, typically requiring a steam host. The cogeneration plant would supply the steam with a byproduct of electrical generation or would supply their own electrical generation with the byproduct being usable steam. When properly designed, cogeneration plants are extremely efficient.

We had just hired a staff engineer named Mike Glancy who was working at one of these small cogeneration facilities in Minnesota. I knew Mike from a few brief encounters with him all the way back at Laramie River Station.

Mike worked for Burns and McDonnell Engineering for several years. He spent almost three years at Bonanza Plant before they moved him to that small cogeneration plant in Mankato, Minnesota. After leaving Bonanza, he realized he loved Vernal and hated Minnesota. Plus, he was fed up with the inescapable nomadic lifestyle required by Burns and McDonnell. Unfortunately, Mike didn't like me, and it was fully justified. It mostly had to do with my old nemesis turned friend, Don Pillar.

Don Pillar didn't like Mike Glancy at all. It is probably accurate to say Don openly hated him. Mike was about 5'2" tall and had serious 'small man syndrome.' Don's arrogance seriously conflicted with Mike's arrogance. Putting the two of them in the same room was akin to a nuclear reaction.

Because Don was the smartest, best powerhouse guy I had ever known and we were now friends, it was my duty to not like Don's enemies, right? Unfortunately, even if I wasn't 12 years old, I certainly acted like I was.

Don treated Mike like crap and even stole his girlfriend. Her name was Trish, and she worked in the warehouse at the plant. In fact, Don did more than steal her, he married her.

I wound up getting in the middle of Mike and Don's feud over Trish, and I took Don's side. This, along with my pettiness and hyper-inflated ego, turned Mike against me... *Hard against me*. Therefore, it was easy for him to mess with my head and send me in the wrong direction.

That morning as I was looking for another plant, I decided to ask Mike about the cogeneration facility he left to come to Vernal. I knew he didn't care for me, but we were civil to each other's faces. I walked over to his office in the engineering area of the admin building.

Leaning in through the door, I quietly asked, "Mike, you got a minute?"

He looked up, frowned, and said, "Only a minute, I've got a ton of stuff to do."

"Mind if I come in and shut the door?" I was trying to portray as much humility as humanly possible.

He paused and grunted, "Fine, make it quick." He was fully underwhelmed at my presence.

I stepped into his office and closed the door. "Tell me about the cogen plant job that you left to come back here." I was keeping my voice low because I didn't want anyone to hear. How foolish was this? I knew Mike didn't like me and was certainly not going to keep this meeting a secret, even if I asked him to do so.

"Why? You think you want to go there or something?" His face lit up, and the frown dissolved into a look of creepy satisfaction.

"Maybe." I paused and lowered my voice even more. "I love start-ups and was curious what the cogeneration scene was like."

"Take a seat, and I will tell you about it." His demeanor was curiously upbeat, and his eyes were now malignantly dancing.

"The company that owns the plant is ADM. This stands for Archer Daniels and Midland. They are the largest grain milling company in the world and they have decided to build several cogeneration plants, including the largest one ever built in the United States."

He exuberantly continued to explain that the plant in Mankato was one of three that needed start-up assistance. These three were in Mankato Minnesota, Des Moines Iowa, and Lincoln Nebraska and were all owned by ADM. They were built by Asea-Stahl in Sweden and were identical, bubbling-bed, multi-bed combustor, fluidized bed units.

He explained that these were the only three in the entire world, and he was working directly with the plants' designers to bring about proof of concept. Burns and McDonnell did the balance of plant design and had the contract for start-up support.

At one point he looked at me with intense fervor in his eyes and said, "You realize that everything is going to fluidized bed technology, right? Frankly, it only makes sense. All the pollution control is completed chemically in the combustion process, so you don't require scrubbers. Plus, all the combustion is kept at 1600° so there are no NOx issues."

He continued for almost 30 minutes discussing fluidized beds and the "amazing" technology in these plants. I may have been an emotional train wreck, but I was still a die-hard powerhouse guy who LOVED technology like this. He took me in, hook, line, and sinker. Okay, I took myself in with him simply and slyly handing me the tools.

He finished by telling me that Burns and McDonnell was using one of their former lead engineers, Steve Swain, as a sourcing agent for contract labor.

I immediately got excited. This was awesome news! I have known Steve Swain since I participated in the LRS start-up. At that time, he was in charge of the plant start-up, and we worked with each other on a limited basis. Mike said Steve lived just outside of Kansas City (Burns and McDonnell headquarters) and started his own company called S-Tech. He was now helping Burns and McDonnell find engineers due to the huge demand they were experiencing from all the cogeneration plants being built. Mike then conveniently gave me Steve's number as we finished talking.

I thanked Mike and wasted no time calling Steve Swain. He remembered me and asked that I send him a current resume as soon as possible. I updated and faxed it to him early that afternoon. He called me back the next morning.

He offered me a contract start-up engineer position. The pay would be $25.00 per hour for every hour worked. All moving and travel expenses would be reimbursed at actual cost. I would also receive a $500.00 a month, tax-free, housing stipend and per-diem at Government published rates for every day I was on a plant site. The per-diem would also be tax-free. He wanted me to start ASAP. I told him I would call him later with my answer.

I didn't even tell anyone I was leaving the plant that morning. I locked my office door and drove straight home to talk to Vangie. Unfortunately, I was loaded for bear, and that poor girl didn't have a chance. I surprised her as I walked into the house.

"What are you doing home?" she asked hesitantly as I enthusiastically walked into the kitchen.

"I need to discuss a job offer I just got." My voice was upbeat, and I was in full-blown salesman mode. She knew immediately I was putting the full-court press on her. We had been married for 13 years, and there were not many surprises between us.

"Wow! You really took a hard fall out there, didn't you?" Her voice was bordering hostile condescension.

I firmly replied, "You need to hear this. It is much better than you think." I paused for effect. "I just talked with Steve Swain. He was a Burns and McDonnell engineer when I was at LRS and now has a company called E-Tech." I proceeded to explain that I would be a start-up engineer and told her about the pay and the benefits. I made sure she knew the per-diem and housing stipend was tax-free.

She suspiciously listened to my overrated diatribe. She didn't trust me in these areas, especially when she knew how depressed I had been since Culligan left.

"Let me see if I understand all of this." We both knew she heard everything that was said, but she was being passive/aggressive with the discussion.

"You are giving up ALL benefits, vacation, sick leave, medical insurance, and retirement to go to work on a contract basis only?" She shook her head and squinted her eyes. "Are you kidding me?" Her beautiful brown eyes were now filled with fire.

I knew I had to sell this better than I currently was doing.

"I will get paid for every hour worked. It is not a salaried position like I have now. The per-diem and housing stipend is tax-free, and we can use it to pay for good medical insurance and still have plenty left to put in the bank."

"How long will we be in Des Moines?" She was transitioning from angry to overwhelmed.

"We will be based in Des Moines for at least a couple of years, but I will have to initially travel to Mankato, Minnesota to finish a start-up there."

"How far is Mankato from Des Moines?"

"About three and a half hours." I knew this wasn't going to go over well.

"So, what are you telling me?" She was transitioning from overwhelmed to exasperated.

"You will be gone all week and come home on weekends, or will you just stay there for a month or two at a time before coming home to visit your children and me?"

"I would come home on Friday nights and leave real early Monday mornings." I was trying to sound as soothing as possible. It was as effective as sweet-talking a mother bear who was guarding her cubs from a dangerous predator.

"You know what?" She shifted from exasperated to inflamed surrender. "Do whatever the hell you want because you are going to do it anyway, and I am sick of you moping around this house and making all our lives miserable." She turned and walked out of the kitchen and into our bedroom, slamming the door extremely hard.

Normally, this would probably win the argument for her. I would back down and apologize. Not this time. I knew I needed to pray and pray hard. Don't get me wrong; there were very few days that I didn't go before the Lord and pray. I would usually time my prayers to ensure I spent at least 30 minutes a day with the Lord. I was earnest and passionate about spending this time every day despite my massive flaws and issues. I knew now I needed to pray as earnestly as I had ever prayed before. I went into the garage and prayed hard for about 20 minutes along these lines…

"Lord, I don't know how I could have messed things up so badly. You had to have seen all this coming. I need to start fresh and not make these same mistakes over again. I need your help right now. I mean, seriously, I REALLY need your help right now. Vangie must accept us moving again, or you need to change my heart and help me ease back into the plant. I need one or the other. I can't continue as I am right now."

Oddly, I finished knowing that regardless of what happened, I had to make things right with Stan Arias and his family. I went back into the house and got my keys, telling Vangie I would be back in a bit. She was still in our bedroom, which wasn't a good sign.

I drove to the Church, hoping Stan would be there. Luckily, he was in his office. I knocked lightly on his open office door. "Can I come in and talk to you?" I asked pensively.

Typical of Stan, he smiled at me and said, "Sure, Mark, what can I do for you?" Maybe it was just my guilt, but his eyes weren't smiling. They just looked pained.

"Stan, I was wrong. I treated you badly, and I have absolutely no excuse." I paused to swallow and choke back some tears. This was proving more emotional than I thought it would. "I'm not sure what came over me, but it was inexcusable, and I want you to know that if I could make it right, I would do so."

"It's okay..." He sighed painfully while trying to portray a semblance of serenity. "I grew from it, so it wasn't a total loss."

"I hope Karen can forgive me. I know how hard this had to be for her."

He tilted his head slightly and, with resignation in his voice said, "She will be fine. I know her feelings were hurt, but she will get over it." He then smiled, and his eyes also smiled this time. "Are you and your family returning to Church with us again?"

We were steadfast givers. We did not 'vote' with our checkbook, as I had seen some people do in the past. If we attended Church somewhere, we tithed there. As small as the World Vision Assembly was, it would be a decent bump to their finances if we returned.

"No. I think we are leaving town. I am taking a job in Iowa." I felt emotionless and empty as I said these words.

"Really?" He seemed a bit puzzled. "You seemed to have such a good job here. Why would you leave?"

"Hard to explain. Essentially, I wasn't just a jerk to you; I seriously burned some bridges at the plant." I then lowered my voice and woefully stated, "I need to start fresh and set a lot of things straight. We need to start over."

He now seemed surprised. "Are you certain this is not an overreaction that will pass?" He paused and lowered his voice, "Or were you let go?"

"No, I wasn't fired. It is just time to leave. I need a fresh start with new people around us so that I can do things right this time."

"I hate to see you go. It sounds like you are already correcting issues based on you coming here to talk to me. Are you certain this is the right move?" I appreciated his words, but they were empty because he didn't know what a mess I had made at the plant. He then raised his eyebrows and, with measured excitement said, "Are you selling your house?"

"If we can. It would definitely be nice to sell it quickly." I was surprised by his inquiry. I hadn't thought much about the house. When I did think about it, I was worried because I knew it would be difficult to sell. The only thing we had going

94

for us was the mortgage, which was a fully assumable FHA mortgage. These were getting harder and harder to come by. The mortgage probably had more value than the house.

Stan lit up, and his eyes widened. "We have a brand-new family in the Church that is looking for a place to live. I don't know their financial situation, but you should talk to them!"

"Absolutely, I would love to discuss it with them. We do really need to sell the house."

We talked for a bit longer, and I apologized to him at least two more times. He was gracious and genuinely accepted my apology. Seeing how considerate and caring he was, comforted me. My pain and regret were sincere.

I finished my conversation with him, and he gave me Emil Padilla's phone number. Stan told me Emil was new to the area, in his mid-40s, worked in the oil patch, and needed a home for his family.

I drove back home, praying continually. I knew something for certain. My heart and mind had not changed about leaving the plant. I wasn't sure what would have happened if Vangie had not had a change of heart. Something had to give, and at this moment, it still wasn't me.

Vangie was back in the kitchen again. I walked in slowly to observe her mood before jumping into anything. She looked stressed but not necessarily angry. This was a good thing.

"Are you okay?" I asked rhetorically.

"I'm fine." She curtly replied.

I decided to slip carefully into sales mode again. "I don't think going to Des Moines will be a bad thing..." Before I could continue, she cut me off.

"Mark, let's get something straight. I don't like it here. I have never liked it here. The only good thing about Vernal is the lakes and the boat." She turned and looked directly at me. "Besides not liking Vernal, I don't particularly want my kids to grow up and marry Mormons."

I shook my head in disbelief. "What's the problem then..."

"The problem is **YOU**." She answered angrily. "This was supposed to be the perfect job. You have straight days, are paid well, and have great benefits." She lowered her voice and continued while barely suppressing her tears. "Are YOU ever going to be happy anywhere?" Before I could give her a lame answer, she continued. "I don't know what you are looking for, but I am afraid you will never find it. How many times are we going to move while looking for something that doesn't exist?"

"You're right." I was taken aback and struggling for the right words. "This was the perfect job, but Culligan leaving like he did completely screwed me."

"Don't you see, something or someone is ALWAYS screwing it up for you? Doesn't that concern you *even a little bit*?"

I was still fixated on her saying she didn't care for Vernal. Amidst this exchange, I saw a light in the form of her maybe agreeing to move to Des Moines. I finally decided to run with it. "Of course, it concerns me, but I don't think it is as bad as what you say."

96

"Whatever." She raised the white flag and groaned with resignation. "Let's just move to Des Moines. However, you had better start thinking about our future. We can't keep moving these kids continuously. It is not healthy for any of us."

"This will work, I promise." I was dumbfounded by her quick surrender and agreement to move to Des Moines.

I went into the front room and called Emil Padilla's number. I reached Emil's wife, Gloria. We talked for a bit, and she was quite excited when I told her that all they would have to do was assume the loan and take over our payments. She assured me that Emil would call me back as soon as he arrived home that day.

As expected, Emil called at about 6:30 that evening, and we talked for over an hour. Obviously, they had no money to put down but would be more than willing to assume the loan and take over our payments if they liked the house. I told them they could come over and look at it at any time.

It is a good thing Vangie always kept a tidy house. They were at our doorstep 15 minutes later. To say they were excited was a massive understatement. They wanted to move forward with the purchase as soon as possible. They were living with a relative, and it sounded like things were quite strained.

The next morning, I typed and submitted my resignation and personally took it to Bob. He looked at it for a few moments before angrily shaking his head and saying, "Someday, you may grow up and make someone a good employee." He tossed the resignation on his desk. "I've got work to do. Please close my door on your way out."

I turned and left, thinking it was going to feel good to give Bob my resignation. It didn't. I felt like the biggest loser ever to walk the face of this earth. It didn't matter. It was now cast in stone. We were moving to Des Moines, IA.

Because selling our home was nothing more than a simple assumption through the FHA, closing took place the day before we left Vernal. No money changed hands between us, but we had to pay some closing costs to ensure it took place. The problem with the simple FHA assumption was glaring. We would still be on the hook if they didn't make their payments. I didn't even know these people, and we were, in effect, co-signing for them to take over our payments. I was worried sick about this but did not see any other way out. We didn't have any equity in the house due to market conditions from the economic downturn in the area.

The fact is, the Padillas only made a couple of payments and then left the area without a forwarding address. We never saw or heard from them again. Did we get stuck with paying off the mortgage after they defaulted?

Believe it or not, we didn't. Vernal was declared an economically impacted area shortly after we left. The Government absorbed the default. It never even showed on our credit report. I cannot tell you what a bullet we dodged on that one. I thank God to this day for that house not being an albatross around our necks.

We moved to Des Moines and started a completely new chapter of life. It was an awful and painful chapter. My uncontrolled and hasty exit from Vernal left gaping wounds in my soul that had to heal. A healing that could not be accomplished without Divine intervention. A healing that eventually occurred, but not without tremendous pain and remorse.

The next few years were, frankly, horrible. I deserved it, and it was obvious I needed some pain to help adjust my way of thinking. Unfortunately, my childishness and idiocy brought pain to my beautiful, amazing wife and kids. In our time in Vernal, I had clearly snatched defeat from the jaws of victory. *Our lives were, once again, changed forever.*

www.ingramcontent.com/pod-product-compliance
Lightning Source LLC
Chambersburg PA
CBHW071026120626
46546CB00003B/1236